COSMETOLOGY
LICENSING EXAM

COSMETOLOGY
LICENSING
EXAM

2nd Edition

NEW YORK

Library of Congress Cataloging-in-Publication Data:
Cosmetology licensing exam.—2nd ed.
        p. cm.
    ISBN 1-57685-413-2
    1. Beauty culture—United States—Examinations, questions, etc. 2. Beauty
Operators—Licenses—United States—Examinations, questions, etc.
I. LearningExpress (Organization)
    TT958 .C67 2003
    646.7'2'076—dc21

                                                            2002012251

Printed in the United States of America
9 8 7 6 5 4 3 2 1
Second Edition

ISBN 1-57685-413-2

For more information or to place an order, contact LearningExpress at:
    900 Broadway
    Suite 604
    New York, NY 10003

Or visit us at:
    www.learnatest.com

Contents

COSMETOLOGY
LICENSING EXAM

1 ▶ The Cosmetology Exam

CHAPTER SUMMARY

This chapter advises you on how to prepare to take the Cosmetology Exam. It outlines the contents of the exam and gives you some tips about how to use this book to study for it.

EACH STATE'S BOARD of cosmetology sets licensure standards for cosmetologists, manicurists, and estheticians. Although requirements and licensure proceedings differ somewhat by state, most require both a written exam and a practical exam, and all are based on the same core content you studied in your cosmetology course.

Over 30 states use the written and practical exams sponsored by the National Interstate Council of State Boards of Cosmetology, Inc. (NIC). Another 18 states use exams sponsored by Experior Assessments, LLC. Both testing companies create exams for state boards of cosmetology that encourage high standards for entry into the profession. Whether your state uses an Experior or an NIC exam, you will be tested on the fundamentals that you learned in your cosmetology course.

A list of specific certification requirements for all 50 states, as well as contact information for the state boards of cosmetology, is found on page 135 of this book.

For more information about NIC and Experior, visit their websites. Both contain helpful information about the organizations, the tests they develop, and the states they serve.

NATIONAL INTERSTATE COUNCIL OF STATE BOARDS OF COSMETOLOGY, INC. (NIC)
P.O. Box 11390
Columbia, SC 29211
www.nictesting.org

EXPERIOR ASSESSMENTS, LLC
1360 Energy Park Drive
St. Paul, MN 55108
www.experioronline.com

▶ The Cosmetology Written Exam

The 100 questions on the Cosmetology Exam are divided into a number of content areas that match the content areas you studied in your cosmetology course. Passing the test means that you have the knowledge required of an entry-level cosmetologist.

Most written examinations for cosmetologists contain questions in four general areas:

- Scientific and Basic Concepts
- Physical Services
- Chemical Services
- Hair Designing

The questions included in the four practice written exams in this book are found in Chapters 3, 5, 6, and 7 and are grouped into these same general categories. So are the additional practice questions that constitute the Cosmetology Refresher Course in Chapter 4. Keep in mind, however, that while the basic content on each exam will be similar, the category groupings can vary from state to state.

The table below shows the content of each practice exam in this book, broken down in a system that is similar to that used for most state exams. The table also lists the subtopics included under each main topic and the number of questions the exams typically contain for those topics. The subtopics will reflect the topics you studied in your cosmetology course and the chapters in your textbook.

Because not all states use the same exam, the exams in this book contain questions that cover all the possible topic areas, such as the business of running a beauty salon, presenting yourself as a professional, and the basics of massage and hair removal. Therefore, no matter what state you live in or what specific content is covered on the exam you take, this book will help you prepare for your exam.

Scientific and Basic Concepts
(30–35 questions per exam)
    Life Skills
    Your Professional Image
    Communicating for Success
    Bacteriology
    Decontamination and Infection Control
    Properties of the Hair and Scalp
    The Nail and Its Disorders
    The Skin and Its Disorders
    Cells, Anatomy, and Physiology
    Electricity and Light Therapy
    Chemistry
    The Salon Business
Physical Services (15–25 questions per exam)
    Draping
    Shampooing, Rinsing, and Conditioning
    Manicuring and Pedicuring
    Advanced Nail Techniques
    Theory of Massage
    Facials
    Facial Makeup
    Hair Removal
Chemical Services (20–30 questions per exam)
    Permanent Waving
    Hair Coloring
    Chemical Hair Relaxing
Hair Design (20–25 questions per exam)
    Haircutting
    Hairstyling
    Thermal Hair Straightening
    Braiding and Braid Extensions
    Wigs and Hair Enhancements

▶ The Practical Exam

Virtually every state board of cosmetology requires a practical exam in addition to the written exam. The content included on the exam varies by state, so you must consult your state board for the specific material that will be included on your exam, as well as exactly how that material will be tested.

Regardless of how your state conducts the practical exam, some content areas are considered essential, either to maintain reciprocity of licensing from state to state, or to meet common job descriptions.

Content areas for the cosmetology practical exam usually include the following key topics:

- Hair Shaping
- Chemical Waving
- Hair Lightening/Hair Coloring
- Chemical Relaxing
- Shaping and Pin Curl Placement
- Thermal Curling
- Blow-Dry Styling

In addition, most states require a number of additions to these subject areas, such as Roller Placement, Facials, Manicuring, and Sculptured Nails.

For each content area in which you are required to demonstrate your competence, you will be given a specific task, all the needed materials, and a time limit. You will be evaluated on your use of proper safety precautions, infection control procedures, and client protection procedures. For example, to demonstrate your competence in chemical waving, you might be directed to wrap the center back section of a head and to section the hair for correct rod placement. You would also be required to demonstrate how to do a test curl. Similar strict guidelines and performance criteria would be given to you for each content area in which you were tested.

Using This Book to Prepare for the Written Test

This book contains 250 review questions in the Cosmetology Refresher Course (Chapter 4), arranged by content grouping, as well as four complete cosmetology practice exams, each containing 100 multiple-choice questions. The practice exam questions are also grouped by content area, since this is the way many state exams are arranged.

The first step in using this book to prepare for your Cosmetology Exam is to read Chapter 2, which presents the nine-step LearningExpress Test Preparation System. This chapter shows you essential test-taking strategies that you can practice as you take the exams in this book.

Your next step is to take the first cosmetology practice exam, Chapter 3, as a pretest. Score your answers using the answer key, which follows the exam. Complete explanations for the answers are included in the key.

Remember, the passing score on most exams is approximately 75%. If you score over 75% on your first practice test, congratulations! Don't assume that this means you will easily pass the actual test without practice. The test questions on the day of your exam may be different from those on the practice test. Although you are well on your way to passing, you will still need some test preparation. No matter what your initial score is, follow the suggestions in the next paragraphs.

If you score less than 75% on Cosmetology Practice Exam 1, don't panic. Do put in some concentrated study time, however. Begin by determining your major areas of weakness. For example, suppose you answered 35 of the pretest questions incorrectly, giving you a score of 65, or 65% correct. On rereading the questions you missed, you find that they break down into the following content areas:

- Scientific and Basic Concepts: you missed 18 out of 36 answers
- Physical Services: you missed 3 out of 23
- Chemical Services: you missed 10 out of 20
- Hair Designing: you missed 3 out of 21

In this example, your analysis tells you that you need to devote extra study time to two areas: Scientific and Basic Concepts and Chemical Services. Try putting in one or two evenings of study specifically on each of these areas. First, check the content breakdown in the table on page 2 to make sure you understand what topics are included in each area. Then review all materials on these topics in your cosmetology textbook and printed materials.

Now that you have taken and analyzed the pretest and reviewed some weak areas, it is time to use Chapter 4, the Cosmetology Refresher Course. Don't treat this 250-question review as a test, even though the questions have been purposely set in the same multiple-choice format of an actual exam.

One strategy for using the Cosmetology Refresher Course is to answer all the questions within one content area (each has a heading) and then review all the answer explanations in that section. Move on to the next section and do the same. This process should reinforce correct answers and immediately modify wrong answers.

Another idea is to take the questions from your weakest content area, and copy them onto flash cards.

Take the flash cards with you wherever you go. If you have some downtime—say waiting for an appointment or in line at the grocery store—you can test yourself with your flashcards.

After you have spent some time on the Cosmetology Refresher Course, you should feel ready to take Practice Exam 2 in Chapter 5. Once again, check your total score and content area breakdown. Chances are that both will have improved.

In the time leading up to the Cosmetology Exam, use the two remaining exams (Chapters 6 and 7) to further pinpoint areas of weakness to review. For example, you may find that now you do very well on all Chemical Services questions except those that concern hair relaxing. That knowledge tells you what specific materials to review.

Once you have worked on and improved your areas of weakness, use the final days before the test to keep fresh and do some general brushing-up on your knowledge and your test-taking skills. Devote a short period of time each day to reviewing several chapters of your textbook. Use the third and fourth practice exams to rehearse test-taking strategies and procedures.

After reading and studying this book, you'll be well on your way to passing the Cosmetology Exam. Good luck as you advance in this rewarding and glamorous career!

CHAPTER

2 ▶ The LearningExpress Test Preparation System

CHAPTER SUMMARY

Taking the Cosmetology Exam can be tough. It demands a lot of preparation if you want to achieve a top score. Your career depends on your passing the exam. The LearningExpress Test Preparation System, developed exclusively for LearningExpress by leading test experts, gives you the discipline and attitude you need to be a winner.

FIRST, THE BAD news: Taking the Cosmetology Exam is no picnic, and neither is getting ready for it. Your future career as a cosmetologist depends on your getting a passing score, but there are all sorts of pitfalls that can keep you from doing your best on this all-important exam. Here are some of the obstacles that can stand in the way of your success:

- Being unfamiliar with the format of the exam
- Being paralyzed by test anxiety
- Leaving your preparation to the last minute
- Not preparing at all!
- Not knowing vital test-taking skills: how to pace yourself through the exam, how to use the process of elimination, and when to guess
- Not being in tip-top mental and physical shape
- Messing up on test day by arriving late at the test site, having to work on an empty stomach, or shivering through the exam because the room is cold

What's the common denominator in all these test-taking pitfalls? One word: control. Who's in control, you or the exam?

Now the good news: The LearningExpress Test Preparation System puts you in control. In just nine easy-to-follow steps, you will learn everything you need to know to make sure that you are in charge of your preparation and your performance on the exam. Other test-takers may let the test get the better of them; other test-takers may be unprepared or out of shape, but not you. You will have taken all the steps you need to take to get a high score on the Cosmetology Exam.

Here's how the LearningExpress Test Preparation System works: Nine easy steps lead you through everything you need to know and do to get ready to master your exam. Each of the steps listed below includes both reading about the step and one or more activities. It's important that you do the activities along with the reading, or you won't be getting the full benefit of the system. Each step tells you approximately how much time that step will take you to complete.

Step 1. Get Information	50 minutes
Step 2. Conquer Test Anxiety	20 minutes
Step 3. Make a Plan	30 minutes
Step 4. Learn to Manage Your Time	10 minutes
Step 5. Learn to Use the Process of Elimination	20 minutes
Step 6. Know When to Guess	20 minutes
Step 7. Reach Your Peak Performance Zone	10 minutes
Step 8. Get Your Act Together	10 minutes
Step 9. Do It!	10 minutes
Total	**3 hours**

We estimate that working through the entire system will take you approximately three hours, though it's perfectly ok if you work faster or slower than the time estimates assume. If you can take an afternoon or evening, you can work through the whole Learning-Express Test Preparation System in one sitting. Other-

wise, you can break it up, and do just one or two steps a day for the next several days. It's up to you—remember, you're in control.

▶ Step 1: Get Information

Time to complete: 50 minutes
Activities: Read Chapter 1, " The Cosmetology Exam" and Chapter 9, " Licensing Requirements"
Knowledge is power. The first step in the LearningExpress Test Preparation System is finding out everything you can about the Cosmetology Exam. Once you have your information, the next steps in the LearningExpress Test Preparation System will show you what to do about it.

Part A: Straight Talk About the Cosmetology Exam

The cosmetology written exam is just one part of a whole series of evaluations you have to go through to show that you are prepared to perform the many, varied tasks of a cosmetologist. The written exam attempts to measure your knowledge of your trade. The practical skills exam attempts to measure your ability to apply what you know.

It's important for you to remember that your score on the cosmetology written exam does not determine how smart you are or even whether you will make a good cosmetologist. There are all kinds of things a written exam like this can't test: whether you are likely to show up late or call in sick a lot, whether you have the interpersonal skills necessary to build the trusting, comfortable relationships that will keep your clients coming back, and whether you have an enthusiastic dedication to learning and performing your trade well. Those kinds of things are hard to evaluate, while your ability to fill in the right little circles on a bubble answer sheet is easy to evaluate.

This is not to say that filling in the right little circles is not important! The knowledge tested on the written exam is knowledge you will need to do your job. And your ability to enter the profession you've trained for depends on your passing this exam. And that's why you're here—using the LearningExpress Test Preparation System to achieve control over the exam.

Part B: What's on the Test

If you haven't already done so, stop here and read Chapter 1 of this book, which gives you an overview of the typical cosmetology written exams.

Always keep in mind that states use different exams. Turn to Chapter 9 for a state-by-state overview of licensing requirements. If you haven't already gotten the full rundown on certification procedures as part of your training program, you can contact the state cosmetology agency listed in Chapter 9 for details.

▶ Step 2: Conquer Test Anxiety

Time to complete: 20 minutes
Activity: Take the Test Stress Test

Having complete information about the exam is the first step in getting control of the exam. Next, you have to overcome one of the biggest obstacles to test success: test anxiety. Test anxiety not only impairs your performance on the exam itself; it can even keep you from preparing! In Step 2, you will learn stress management techniques that will help you succeed on your exam. Learn these strategies now, and practice them as you work through the exams in this book, so they'll be second nature to you by exam day.

Combating Test Anxiety

The first thing you need to know is that a little test anxiety is a good thing. Everyone gets nervous before a big exam—and if that nervousness motivates you to prepare thoroughly, so much the better. It's said that Sir Laurence Olivier, one of the foremost British actors of this century, threw up before every performance. His stage fright didn't impair his performance; in fact, it

probably gave him a little extra edge—just the kind of edge you need to do well, whether on a stage or in an examination room.

On the next page is the Test Stress Test. Stop here and answer these questions to find out whether your level of test anxiety is something you should worry about.

Stress Management Before the Test

If you feel your level of anxiety getting the best of you in the weeks before the test, here is what you need to do to bring the level down again:

- **Get prepared.** There's nothing like knowing what to expect and being prepared for it to put you in control of test anxiety. That's why you're reading this book. Use it faithfully, and remind yourself that you're better prepared than most of the people taking the test.
- **Practice self-confidence.** A positive attitude is a great way to combat test anxiety. This is no time to be humble or shy. Stand in front of the mirror and say to your reflection, "I'm prepared. I'm full of self-confidence. I'm going to ace this test. I know I can do it." Say it into a tape recorder and play it back once a day. If you hear it often enough, you will believe it.
- **Fight negative messages.** Every time someone starts telling you how hard the exam is or how it's almost impossible to get a high score, start telling them your self-confidence messages above. If the someone with the negative messages is you, telling yourself you don't do well on exams, you just can't do this, don't listen. Turn on your tape recorder and listen to your self-confidence messages.
- **Visualize.** Imagine yourself reporting for duty on your first day as a cosmetologist. Think of yourself at a fashion shoot, styling hair and making up faces of top models—you're part of the action. Visualizing success can help make it happen—

Test Stress Test

You only need to worry about test anxiety if it is extreme enough to impair your performance. The following questionnaire will provide a diagnosis of your level of test anxiety. In the blank before each statement, write the number that most accurately describes your experience.

0 = Never
1 = Once or twice
2 = Sometimes
3 = Often

____I have gotten so nervous before an exam that I simply put down the books and didn't study for it.

____I have experienced disabling physical symptoms such as vomiting and severe headaches because I was nervous about an exam.

____I have simply not showed up for an exam because I was scared to take it.

____I have experienced dizziness and disorientation while taking an exam.

____I have had trouble filling in the little circles because my hands were shaking too hard.

____I have failed an exam because I was too nervous to complete it.

____**Total: Add up the numbers in the blanks above.**

Your Test Stress Score

Here are the steps you should take, depending on your score. If you scored:

- **Below 3**, your level of test anxiety is nothing to worry about; it's probably just enough to give you that little extra edge.
- **Between 3 and 6**, your test anxiety may be enough to impair your performance, and you should practice the stress management techniques listed in this section to try to bring your test anxiety down to manageable levels.
- **Above 6**, your level of test anxiety is a serious concern. In addition to practicing the stress management techniques listed in this section, you may want to seek additional, personal help. Call your local high school or community college and ask for the academic counselor. Tell the counselor that you have a level of test anxiety that sometimes keeps you from being able to take the exam. The counselor may be willing to help you or may suggest someone else you should talk to.

and it reminds you of why you're going through all this work in preparing for the exam.

- **Exercise.** Physical activity helps calm your body down and focus your mind. Besides, being in good physical shape can actually help you do well on the exam. Go for a run, lift weights, go swimming—and do it regularly.

Stress Management on Test Day

There are several ways you can bring down your level of test anxiety on test day. These methods work best if you practice them in the weeks before the test, so you know which ones work for you.

- **Deep breathing.** Take a deep breath while you count to five. Hold it for a count of one, then let it out on a count of five. Repeat several times.
- **Move your body.** Try rolling your head in a circle. Rotate your shoulders. Shake your hands from the wrist. Many people find these movements very relaxing.
- **Visualize again.** Think of the place where you are most relaxed: lying on the beach in the sun, walking through the park, or whatever. Now close your eyes and imagine you're actually there. If you practice in advance, you'll find that you only need a few seconds of this exercise to experience a significant increase in your sense of well-being.

When anxiety threatens to overwhelm you right there during the exam, there are still things you can do to manage the stress level:

- **Repeat your self-confidence messages.** You should have them memorized by now. Say them quietly to yourself, and believe them!
- **Visualize one more time.** This time, visualize yourself moving smoothly and quickly through the test, answering every question right, and finishing just before time is up. Like most visualiza-

tion techniques, this one works best if you've practiced it ahead of time.

- **Find an easy question.** Skim over the test until you find an easy question, and answer it. Getting even one circle filled in gets you into the test-taking groove.
- **Take a mental break.** Everyone loses concentration once in a while during a long test. It's normal, so you shouldn't worry about it. Instead, accept what has happened. Say to yourself, "Hey, I lost it there for a minute. My brain is taking a break." Put down your pencil, close your eyes, and do some deep breathing for a few seconds. Then you're ready to go back to work.

Try these techniques ahead of time, and see if they work for you!

▶ Step 3: Make a Plan

Time to complete: 30 minutes
Activity: Construct a study plan
Maybe the most important thing you can do to get control of yourself and your exam is to make a study plan. Too many people fail to prepare simply because they fail to plan. Spending hours on the day before the exam poring over sample test questions not only raises your level of test anxiety, it also is simply no substitute for careful preparation and practice over time.

Don't fall into the cram trap. Take control of your preparation time by mapping out a study schedule. On the following pages are two sample schedules, based on the amount of time you have before you take the Cosmetology written exam. If you're the kind of person who needs deadlines and assignments to motivate you for a project, here they are. If you're the kind of person who doesn't like to follow other people's plans, you can use the suggested schedules here to construct your own.

Even more important than making a plan is making a commitment. You can't review everything you learned in your Cosmetology course in one night. You have to set aside some time every day for study and practice. Try for at least 20 minutes a day. Twenty minutes daily will do you much more good than two hours on Saturday.

Don't put off your study until the day before the exam. Start now. A few minutes a day, with half an hour or more on weekends, can make a big difference in your score.

Schedule A: The 30-Day plan

If you have at least a month before you take the Cosmetology exam, you have plenty of time to prepare—as long as you don't waste it! If you have less than a month, turn to Schedule B.

TIME	PREPARATION
Days 1–4	Skim over the written materials from your training program, particularly noting 1) areas you expect to be emphasized on the exam and 2) areas you don't remember well. On Day 4, concentrate on those areas.
Day 5	Take the first practice exam found in Chapter 3.
Day 6	Score the first practice exam. Use the outline of skills on the test given in Chapter 1 to show you which are your strongest and weakest areas. Identify two areas that you will concentrate on before you take the second practice exam.
Days 7–10	Study the two areas you identified as your weak points. Use the Refresher Course in Chapter 4 for extra practice in these areas.
Day 11	Take the second practice exam in Chapter 5.
Day 12	Score the second practice exam. Identify one area to concentrate on before you take the third practice exam.
Days 13–18	Study the one area you identified for review. Again, use the Refresher Course in Chapter 4 for extra practice in this area.

TIME	PREPARATION
Day 19	Take the third practice exam found in Chapter 6.
Day 20	Once again, identify one area to review, based on your score on the third practice exam.
Days 20–21	Study the one area you identified for review, using the Refresher Course in Chapter 4 for extra practice.
Days 22–25	Take an overview of all your training materials, consolidating your strengths and improving on your weaknesses.
Days 26–27	Review all the areas that have given you the most trouble in the three practice exams you've taken so far.
Day 28	Take the fourth practice exam in Chapter 7. Note how much you've improved!
Day 29	Review one or two weak areas, doing any sample questions in these areas from Chapter 4 that you haven't already done.
Day before the exam	Relax. Do something unrelated to the exam and go to bed at a reasonable hour.

Schedule B: The 10-Day Plan

If you have two weeks or less before you take the exam, you may have your work cut out for you. Use this 10-day schedule to help you make the most of your time.

TIME	PREPARATION
Day 1	Take the first practice exam in Chapter 3 and score it using the answer key at the end. Turn to the list of subject areas on the exam in Chapter 1, and find out which areas need the most work, based on your exam score.
Day 2	Review one area that gave you trouble on the first practice exam. Use the Refresher Course in Chapter 4 for extra practice in these areas.
Day 3	Review another area that gave you trouble on the first practice exam. Again, use the questions in Chapter 4 for extra practice.
Day 4	Take the second practice exam in Chapter 5 and score it.
Day 5	If your score on the second practice exam doesn't show improvement on the two areas you studied, review them. If you did improve in those areas, choose a new weak area to study today.

TIME	PREPARATION
Day 6	Take the third practice exam in Chapter 6 and score it.
Day 7	Choose your weakest area from the third practice exam to review. Use the Refresher Course in Chapter 4 for extra practice.
Day 8	Review any areas that you have not yet covered in this schedule.
Day 9	Take the fourth practice exam in Chapter 7 and score it.
Day 10	Use your last study day to brush up on any areas that are still giving you trouble. Do any sample questions in those areas from Chapter 4 that you haven't already done.
Day before the exam	Relax. Do something unrelated to the exam and go to bed at a reasonable hour.

▶ Step 4: Learn to Manage Your Time

Time to complete: 10 minutes to read, many hours of practice!

Activities: Practice these strategies as you take the sample tests in this book

Steps 4, 5, and 6 of the LearningExpress Test Preparation System put you in charge of your exam by showing you test-taking strategies that work. Practice these strategies as you take the sample tests in this book, and then you'll be ready to use them on test day.

First, you will take control of your time on the exam. Most cosmetology exams have a time limit, which may give you more than enough time to complete all the questions—or may not. It's a terrible feeling to hear the examiner say, "Five minutes left," when you're only three-quarters of the way through the test. Here are some tips to keep that from happening to you.

- **Follow directions.** If the directions are given orally, listen to them. If they're written on the exam booklet, read them carefully. Ask questions before the exam begins if there's anything you don't understand. If you're allowed to write in your exam booklet, write down the beginning time and the ending time of the exam.
- **Pace yourself.** Glance at your watch every few minutes, and compare the time to how far you've gotten in the test. When one-quarter of the time has elapsed, you should be a quarter of the way through the test, and so on. If you're falling behind, pick up the pace a bit.
- **Keep moving.** Don't dither around on one question. If you don't know the answer, skip the question and move on. Circle the number of the question in your test booklet in case you have time to come back to it later.
- **Keep track of your place on the answer sheet.** If you skip a question, make sure you skip on the answer sheet too. Check yourself every 5–10 questions to make sure the question number and the answer sheet number are still the same.
- **Don't rush.** Though you should keep moving, rushing won't help. Try to keep calm and work methodically and quickly.

▶ Step 5: Learn to Use the Process of Elimination

Time to complete: 20 minutes

Activity: Complete worksheet on Using the Process of Elimination

After time management, your next most important tool for taking control of your exam is using the process of elimination wisely. It's standard test-taking wisdom that you should always read all the answer choices before choosing your answer. This helps you find the right answer by eliminating wrong answer choices. And, sure enough, that standard wisdom applies to your exam, too.

Let's say you're facing a question that goes like this:

12. Trichology is the study of
   a. hair.
   b. beauty.
   c. magic.
   d. cards.

You should always use the process of elimination on a question like this, even if the right answer jumps out at you. Sometimes the answer that jumps out isn't right after all. Let's assume, for the purpose of this exercise, that you're a little rusty on your terminology, so you need to use a little intuition to make up for what you don't remember. Proceed through the answer choices in order.

So, you start with answer a. "Hair" looks like a good choice; after all, a good deal of what you study has to do with hair, and the word trichology sounds very familiar to you. Put a check mark next to choice a, meaning "good answer, I might use this one."

On to the next. "Beauty" looks good since beauty is another subject you've studied in depth. But you know that words associated with beauty usually begin with belle or beau. Put a question mark next to b, meaning "well, maybe."

Choice c doesn't seem likely. Why would the test makers ask you a question about magic? Put an X next to this one so you never have to look at it again.

Choice d seems just as unlikely. What do cards have to do with being a cosmetologist? It's safe to put an X next to this one too.

Now your question looks like this:

12. Trichology is the study of
✓ a.　　hair
? b.　　beauty
X c.　　magic
X d.　　cards

You've got just one check mark, for a good answer. If you're pressed for time, you should simply mark answer a on your answer sheet. If you've got the time to be extra careful, you could compare your check-mark answer to your question-mark answers to make sure that it's better.

It's good to have a system for marking good, bad, and maybe answers. We recommend this one:

X = bad
✓ = good
? = maybe

If you don't like these marks, devise your own system. Just make sure you do it long before test day—while you're working through the practice exams in this book—so you won't have to worry about it during the test.

Even when you think you're absolutely clueless about a question, you can often use process of elimination to get rid of one answer choice. If so, you're better prepared to make an educated guess, as you'll see in Step 6. More often, the process of elimination allows you to get down to only two possibly right answers. Then you're in a strong position to guess. And sometimes, even though you don't know the right answer, you find it simply by getting rid of the wrong ones, as you did in the example above.

Try using your powers of elimination on the questions in the worksheet Using the Process of Elimination below. The questions aren't about cosmetology work; they're just designed to show you how the process of elimination works. The answer explanations for this worksheet show one possible way you might use the process to arrive at the right answer.

The process of elimination is your tool for the next step, which is knowing when to guess.

▶ Step 6: Know When to Guess

Time to complete: 20 minutes
Activity: Complete worksheet on Your Guessing Ability
Armed with the process of elimination, you're ready to take control of one of the big questions in test-taking: Should I guess? The first and main answer is Yes. Some exams have what's called a "guessing penalty," in which a fraction of your wrong answers is subtracted from your right answers—but cosmetology exams don't tend to work like that. The number of questions you answer correctly yields your raw score. So, you have nothing to lose and everything to gain by guessing.

The more complicated answer to the question "Should I guess?" depends on you—your personality and your "guessing intuition." There are two things you need to know about yourself before you go into the exam:

Using the Process of Elimination

Use the process of elimination to answer the following questions.

1. Ilsa is as old as Meghan will be in five years. The difference between Ed's age and Meghan's age is twice the difference between Ilsa's age and Meghan's age. Ed is 29. How old is Ilsa?
   - a. 4
   - b. 10
   - c. 19
   - d. 24

2. "All drivers of commercial vehicles must carry a valid commercial driver's license whenever operating a commercial vehicle."

   According to this sentence, which of the following people need **NOT** carry a commercial driver's license?
   - a. a truck driver idling his engine while waiting to be directed to a loading dock
   - b. a bus operator backing her bus out of the way of another bus in the bus lot
   - c. a taxi driver driving his personal car to the grocery store
   - d. a limousine driver taking the limousine to her home after dropping off her last passenger of the evening

3. Smoking tobacco has been linked to
   - a. increased risk of stroke and heart attack.
   - b. all forms of respiratory disease.
   - c. increasing mortality rates over the past ten years.
   - d. juvenile delinquency.

4. Which of the following words is spelled correctly?
   - a. incorrigible
   - b. outragous
   - c. domestickated
   - d. understandible

Answers

Here are the answers, as well as some suggestions as to how you might have used the process of elimination to find them.

1. **d**. You should have eliminated answer **a** right off the bat. Ilsa can't be four years old if Meghan is going to be Ilsa's age in five years. The best way to eliminate other answer choices is to try plugging them in to the information given in the problem. For instance, for answer **b**, if Ilsa is 10, then Meghan must be 5. The difference between their ages is 5. The difference between Ed's age, 29, and Meghan's age, 5, is 24. Is 24 two times 5? No. Then answer **b** is wrong. You could eliminate answer **c** in the same way and be left with answer **d**.

2. **c**. Note the word *not* in the question, and go through the answers one by one. Is the truck driver in choice **a** "operating a commercial vehicle"? Yes, idling counts as "operating," so he needs to have a commercial driver's license. Likewise, the bus operator in answer **b** is operating a commercial vehicle; the question doesn't say the operator has to be on the street. The limo driver in choice **d** is operating a commercial vehicle, even if it doesn't have a passenger in it. However, the cabbie in answer **c** is not operating a commercial vehicle, but his own private car.

3. **a**. You could eliminate answer **b** simply because of the presence of the word *all*. Such absolutes hardly ever appear in correct answer choices. Choice **c** looks attractive until you think a little about what you know—aren't fewer people smoking these days, rather than more? So how could smoking be responsible for a higher mortality rate? (If you didn't know that mortality rate means the rate at which

people die, you might keep this choice as a possibility, but you would still be able to eliminate two answers and have only two to choose from.) And choice **d** is plain silly, so you could eliminate that one too. You are left with the correct choice, **a**.

4. a. How you used the process of elimination here depends on which words you recognized as being spelled incorrectly. If you knew that the correct spellings were outrageous, domesticated, and understandable, then you were home free. Surely you knew that at least one of those words was wrong!

Your Guessing Ability

The following are ten really hard questions. You are not supposed to know the answers. Rather, this is an assessment of your ability to guess when you don't have a clue. Read each question carefully, as if you were expected to answer it. If you have any knowledge of the subject, use that knowledge to help you eliminate wrong answer choices.

1. September 7 is Independence Day in
  a. India
  b. Costa Rica
  c. Brazil
  d. Australia

2. Which of the following is the formula for determining the momentum of an object?
  a. $p = MV$
  b. $F = ma$
  c. $P = IV$
  d. $E = mc^2$

3. Because of the expansion of the universe, the stars and other celestial bodies are all moving away from each other. This phenomenon is known as
  a. Newton's first law
  b. the big bang
  c. gravitational collapse
  d. Hubble flow

4. American author Gertrude Stein was born in
  a. 1713
  b. 1830
  c. 1874
  d. 1901

5. Which of the following is **NOT** one of the Five Classics attributed to Confucius?
  a. the I Ching
  b. the Book of Holiness
  c. the Spring and Autumn Annals
  d. the Book of History

6. The religious and philosophical doctrine that holds that the universe is constantly in a struggle between good and evil is known as
  a. Pelagianism
  b. Manichaeanism
  c. neo-Hegelianism
  d. Epicureanism

7. The third Chief Justice of the U.S. Supreme Court was
  a. John Blair
  b. William Cushing
  c. James Wilson
  d. John Jay

8. Which of the following is the poisonous portion of a daffodil?
   a. the bulb
   b. the leaves
   c. the stem
   d. the flowers

9. The winner of the Masters golf tournament in 1953 was
   a. Sam Snead.
   b. Cary Middlecoff.
   c. Arnold Palmer.
   d. Ben Hogan.

10. The state with the highest per capita personal income in 1980 was
   a. Alaska.
   b. Connecticut.
   c. New York.
   d. Texas.

Answers

Check your answers against the correct answers below.
   1. c.
   2. a.
   3. d.
   4. c.
   5. b.
   6. b.
   7. b.
   8. a.
   9. d.
   10. a.

How Did You Do?

You may have simply gotten lucky and actually known the answer to one or two questions. In addition, your guessing was probably more successful if you were able to use the process of elimination on any of the questions. Maybe you didn't know who the third Chief Justice was (question 7), but you knew that John Jay was the first. In that case, you would have eliminated answer **d** and, therefore, improved your odds of guessing right from one in four to one in three.

According to probability, you should get two and a half answers correct, so getting either two or three right would be average. If you got four or more right, you may be a really terrific guesser. If you got one or none right, you may be a really bad guesser.

Keep in mind, though, that this is only a small sample. You should continue to keep track of your guessing ability as you work through the sample questions in this book. Circle the numbers of questions you guess on as you make your guess; or, if you don't have time while you take the practice tests, go back afterward and try to remember which questions you guessed at. Remember, on a test with four answer choices, your chance of guessing correctly is one in four. So keep a separate "guessing" score for each exam. How many questions did you guess on? How many did you get right? If the number you got right is at least one-fourth of the number of questions you guessed on, you are at least an average guesser—maybe better—and you should always go ahead and guess on the real exam. If the number you got right is significantly lower than one-fourth of the number you guessed on, you need to improve your guessing skills.

- Are you a risk-taker?
- Are you a good guesser?

You will have to decide about your risk-taking quotient on your own. To find out if you're a good guesser, complete the worksheet **Your Guessing Ability**. Frankly, even if you're a play-it-safe person with lousy intuition, you're still safe in guessing every time. The best thing would be if you could overcome your anxieties and go ahead and mark an answer. But you may want to have a sense of how good your intuition is before you go into the exam.

▶ Step 7: Reach Your Peak Performance Zone

Time to complete: 10 minutes to read; weeks to complete!
Activity: Complete the Physical Preparation Checklist
To get ready for a challenge like a big exam, you have to take control of your physical, as well as your mental, state. Exercise, proper diet, and rest will ensure that your body works with, rather than against, your mind on test day, as well as during your preparation.

Exercise
If you don't already have a regular exercise program going, the time during which you're preparing for an exam is actually an excellent time to start one. And if you're already keeping fit—or trying to get that way—don't let the pressure of preparing for an exam fool you into quitting now. Exercise helps reduce stress by pumping wonderful good-feeling hormones called endorphins into your system. It also increases the oxygen supply throughout your body, including your brain, so you'll be at peak performance on test day.

A half hour of vigorous activity—enough to raise a sweat—every day should be your aim. If you're really pressed for time, every other day is OK. Choose an activity you like and get out there and do it. Jogging with a friend always makes the time go faster, or take a radio.

But don't overdo it. You don't want to exhaust yourself. Moderation is the key.

Diet
First of all, cut out the junk. Go easy on caffeine and nicotine, and eliminate alcohol and any other drugs from your system at least two weeks before the exam. Promise yourself a binge the night after the exam, if need be.

What your body needs for peak performance is simply a balanced diet. Eat plenty of fruits and vegetables, along with protein and carbohydrates. Foods that are high in lecithin (an amino acid), such as fish and beans, are especially good "brain foods."

The night before the exam, you might "carbo-load" the way athletes do before a contest. Eat a big plate of spaghetti, rice and beans, or whatever your favorite carbohydrate is.

Rest
You probably know how much sleep you need every night to be at your best, even if you don't always get it. Make sure you do get that much sleep, though, for at least a week before the exam. Moderation is important here, too. Extra sleep will just make you groggy.

If you're not a morning person and your exam will be given in the morning, you should reset your internal clock so that your body doesn't think you're taking an exam at 3 A.M. You have to start this process well before the exam. The way it works is to get up half an hour earlier each morning, and then go to bed half an hour earlier that night. Don't try it the other way around; you'll just toss and turn if you go to bed early without having gotten up early. The next morning, get up another half an hour earlier, and so on. How long you will have to do this depends on how late you're used to getting up. Use the Physical Preparation Checklist on the next page to make sure you're in tip-top form.

Physical Preparation Checklist

For the week before the test, write down 1) what physical exercise you engaged in and for how long and 2) what you ate for each meal. Remember, you're trying for at least half an hour of exercise every other day (preferably every day) and a balanced diet that's light on junk food.

Exam minus 7 days

Exercise: _____ for _____ minutes

Breakfast: _____

Lunch: _____

Dinner: _____

Snacks: _____

Exam minus 6 days

Exercise: _____ for _____ minutes

Breakfast: _____

Lunch: _____

Dinner: _____

Snacks: _____

Exam minus 5 days

Exercise: _____ for _____ minutes

Breakfast: _____

Lunch: _____

Dinner: _____

Snacks: _____

Exam minus 4 days

Exercise: _____ for _____ minutes

Breakfast: _____

Lunch: _____

Dinner: _____

Snacks: _____

Exam minus 3 days

Exercise: _____ for _____ minutes

Breakfast: _____

Lunch: _____

Dinner: _____

Snacks: _____

Exam minus 2 days

Exercise: _____ for _____ minutes

Breakfast: _____

Lunch: _____

Dinner: _____

Snacks: _____

Exam minus 1 day

Exercise: _____ for _____ minutes

Breakfast: _____

Lunch: _____

Dinner: _____

Snacks: _____

▶ Step 8: Get Your Act Together

Time to complete: 10 minutes to read; time to complete will vary
Activity: Complete Final Preparations worksheet
You're in control of your mind and body; you're in charge of test anxiety, your preparation, and your test-taking strategies. Now it's time to take charge of external factors, like the testing site and the materials you need to take the exam.

Find Out Where the Test Is and Make a Trial Run

The testing agency or your cosmetology instructor will notify you when and where your exam is being held. Do you know how to get to the testing site? Do you know how long it will take to get there? If not, make a trial run, preferably on the same day of the week at the same time of day. Make note, on the worksheet Final Preparations on page 20, of the amount of time it will take you to get to the exam site. Plan on arriving 10–15 minutes early so you can get the lay of the land, use the bathroom, and calm down. Then figure out how early you will have to get up that morning, and make sure you get up that early every day for a week before the exam.

Gather Your Materials

The night before the exam, lay out the clothes you will wear and the materials you have to bring with you to the exam. Plan on dressing in layers; you won't have any control over the temperature of the examination room. Have a sweater or jacket you can take off if it's warm. Use the checklist on the worksheet **Final Preparations** to help you pull together what you'll need.

Don't Skip Breakfast

Even if you don't usually eat breakfast, do so on exam morning. A cup of coffee doesn't count. Don't eat doughnuts or other sweet foods, either. A sugar high will leave you with a sugar low in the middle of the exam. A mix of protein and carbohydrates is best: cereal with milk and just a little sugar, or eggs with toast, will do your body a world of good.

▶ Step 9: Do It!

Time to complete: 10 minutes, plus test-taking time
Activity: Ace the Cosmetology Exam!
Fast forward to exam day. You're ready. You made a study plan and followed through. You practiced your test-taking strategies while working through this book. You're in control of your physical, mental, and emotional state. You know when and where to show up and what to bring with you. In other words, you're better prepared than most of the other people taking the Cosmetology Exam with you. You're psyched.

Just one more thing. When you're done with the exam, you will have earned a reward. Plan a celebration. Call up your friends and plan a party, or have a nice dinner for two—whatever your heart desires. Give yourself something to look forward to.

And then do it. Go into the exam, full of confidence, armed with test-taking strategies you've practiced until they're second nature. You're in control of yourself, your environment, and your performance on the exam. You're ready to succeed. So do it. Go in there and ace the exam. And look forward to your future career as a cosmetologist!

Final Preparations

Getting to the Exam Site

Location of exam site: _____

Date: _____

Departure time: _____

Do I know how to get to the exam site?   Yes____   No ____   (If no, make a trial run.)

Time it will take to get to exam site: _____

Things to Lay Out the Night Before

Clothes I will wear   ____

Sweater/jacket   ____

Watch   ____

Photo ID   ____

No. 2 pencils   ____

_____   ____

_____   ____

3 ▶ Cosmetology Practice Exam 1

CHAPTER SUMMARY

This is the first of four practice exams based on the core content of your cosmetology coursework. Use this exam as a "pretest." Like the other tests in this book, Exam 1 is based on the cosmetology subjects tested throughout the United States. See Chapter 1 for additional information on the exam.

NOW THAT YOU have studied the LearningExpress Test Preparation System, you are ready to take Cosmetology Practice Exam 1. Most cosmetology exams are timed, but for now, don't worry about how long you take to answer the questions. Try to relax. You can practice under timed conditions with the other practice exams in this book.

The answer sheet is on the following page, followed by the exam. The correct answers, each fully explained, follow the exam. When you have read and understood all the answers, turn back to Chapter 1 for an explanation of how to score and analyze your exam. You will then determine possible weak areas to study further in Chapter 4, The Cosmetology Refresher Course.

COSMETOLOGY ANSWER SHEET

Practice Exam 1

1.	(a) (b) (c) (d)	36.	(a) (b) (c) (d)	71.	(a) (b) (c) (d)
2.	(a) (b) (c) (d)	37.	(a) (b) (c) (d)	72.	(a) (b) (c) (d)
3.	(a) (b) (c) (d)	38.	(a) (b) (c) (d)	73.	(a) (b) (c) (d)
4.	(a) (b) (c) (d)	39.	(a) (b) (c) (d)	74.	(a) (b) (c) (d)
5.	(a) (b) (c) (d)	40.	(a) (b) (c) (d)	75.	(a) (b) (c) (d)
6.	(a) (b) (c) (d)	41.	(a) (b) (c) (d)	76.	(a) (b) (c) (d)
7.	(a) (b) (c) (d)	42.	(a) (b) (c) (d)	77.	(a) (b) (c) (d)
8.	(a) (b) (c) (d)	43.	(a) (b) (c) (d)	78.	(a) (b) (c) (d)
9.	(a) (b) (c) (d)	44.	(a) (b) (c) (d)	79.	(a) (b) (c) (d)
10.	(a) (b) (c) (d)	45.	(a) (b) (c) (d)	80.	(a) (b) (c) (d)
11.	(a) (b) (c) (d)	46.	(a) (b) (c) (d)	81.	(a) (b) (c) (d)
12.	(a) (b) (c) (d)	47.	(a) (b) (c) (d)	82.	(a) (b) (c) (d)
13.	(a) (b) (c) (d)	48.	(a) (b) (c) (d)	83.	(a) (b) (c) (d)
14.	(a) (b) (c) (d)	49.	(a) (b) (c) (d)	84.	(a) (b) (c) (d)
15.	(a) (b) (c) (d)	50.	(a) (b) (c) (d)	85.	(a) (b) (c) (d)
16.	(a) (b) (c) (d)	51.	(a) (b) (c) (d)	86.	(a) (b) (c) (d)
17.	(a) (b) (c) (d)	52.	(a) (b) (c) (d)	87.	(a) (b) (c) (d)
18.	(a) (b) (c) (d)	53.	(a) (b) (c) (d)	88.	(a) (b) (c) (d)
19.	(a) (b) (c) (d)	54.	(a) (b) (c) (d)	89.	(a) (b) (c) (d)
20.	(a) (b) (c) (d)	55.	(a) (b) (c) (d)	90.	(a) (b) (c) (d)
21.	(a) (b) (c) (d)	56.	(a) (b) (c) (d)	91.	(a) (b) (c) (d)
22.	(a) (b) (c) (d)	57.	(a) (b) (c) (d)	92.	(a) (b) (c) (d)
23.	(a) (b) (c) (d)	58.	(a) (b) (c) (d)	93.	(a) (b) (c) (d)
24.	(a) (b) (c) (d)	59.	(a) (b) (c) (d)	94.	(a) (b) (c) (d)
25.	(a) (b) (c) (d)	60.	(a) (b) (c) (d)	95.	(a) (b) (c) (d)
26.	(a) (b) (c) (d)	61.	(a) (b) (c) (d)	96.	(a) (b) (c) (d)
27.	(a) (b) (c) (d)	62.	(a) (b) (c) (d)	97.	(a) (b) (c) (d)
28.	(a) (b) (c) (d)	63.	(a) (b) (c) (d)	98.	(a) (b) (c) (d)
29.	(a) (b) (c) (d)	64.	(a) (b) (c) (d)	99.	(a) (b) (c) (d)
30.	(a) (b) (c) (d)	65.	(a) (b) (c) (d)	100.	(a) (b) (c) (d)
31.	(a) (b) (c) (d)	66.	(a) (b) (c) (d)		
32.	(a) (b) (c) (d)	67.	(a) (b) (c) (d)		
33.	(a) (b) (c) (d)	68.	(a) (b) (c) (d)		
34.	(a) (b) (c) (d)	69.	(a) (b) (c) (d)		
35.	(a) (b) (c) (d)	70.	(a) (b) (c) (d)		

118. If you accidentally cut your client's skin during a manicure, you should
a. apply a weak hydrogen peroxide solution or powdered alum.
b. advise the client to wash her hands with soap and water.
c. apply an adhesive bandage and do not polish the nail on that finger.
d. file an incident report and offer to call a doctor.

119. If it is necessary to cut a client's cuticles to remove them, you should be careful to
a. remove a portion of epidermis as well.
b. cut extremely close to the epidermis.
c. remove the cuticle in a single piece.
d. use a straight razor with a dull edge.

120. If a hand massage is given as part of a manicure, it is done before
a. nail shaping.
b. soaking.
c. the base coat.
d. the top coat.

121. When giving a leg massage,
a. use firm pressure over the shinbone.
b. massage the calf muscles with an upward movement.
c. end about halfway between the knee and the groin.
d. massage both legs at once.

122. A client asks you to trim away a corn that is causing her discomfort. You should
a. refer her to a physician or podiatrist.
b. refer her to an orthopedic surgeon.
c. ask your supervisor for permission.
d. do as the client requests immediately.

Advanced Nail Techniques

123. The purpose of roughing up the existing nail surface before nail wrapping is to
a. make the wrap adhere better.
b. remove diseased tissue.
c. make the nail as short as possible.
d. cause the existing nail to fall off sooner.

124. Sculptured nails are also known as
a. wrapped nails.
b. built-on nails.
c. designer nails.
d. artificial nails.

125. Which statement about artificial nails is correct?
a. Artificial nails can be worn for up to two months at a time.
b. Artificial nails are not flammable.
c. Artificial nails should not be immersed in water for long periods of time.
d. Artificial nails can be immersed in water for long periods of time without loosening.

126. Which statement about nail tipping is correct?
a. Nail tips are used to correct broken or cracked nails.
b. When affixing nail tips, apply adhesive to the underside of the natural nail.
c. Nail tips are removed by filing down to the natural nail.
d. The nail tip is sized and shaped to fit the free edge of the client's nail.

127. How far down should the nail tip cover?
a. one-quarter of the natural nail plate
b. one-half of the natural nail plate
c. two-thirds of the natural nail plate
d. one-third of the natural nail plate

128. Before applying the nail tip you must first apply what to the nail?
a. antiseptic
b. primer
c. adhesive
d. bonding glue

129. Nail tips are removed by soaking the nails in
a. colored polish.
b. clear polish.
c. warm water.
d. acetone.

130. A nail wrap system that is a polish made with tiny fibers designed to strengthen and preserve the natural nail as it grows is called a
a. liquid nail wrap.
b. a nail adhesive.
c. a strengthener.
d. a ridge filler.

131. What two products must be combined in order to have acrylic nails?
a. powder and polish
b. acetone and acrylic
c. acrylic and polish
d. powder and acrylic

132. The substance that improves adhesion and prepares the nail surface for bonding with the acrylic material is called a
a. primer.
b. adhesive.
c. powder.
d. spray.

Theory Of Massage

133. A kneading movement used in massage is
a. petrissage.
b. friction.
c. effleurage.
d. percussion.

134. The most stimulating massage movement is
a. petrissage.
b. friction.
c. effleurage.
d. percussion.

135. Percussion movements to the face should consist of
a. light finger taps.
b. medium finger taps.
c. light knuckle raps.
d. medium knuckle raps.

136. You should **NOT** massage a client who has
a. arthritis.
b. heart or circulatory disease.
c. diabetes.
d. Alzheimer's disease or other dementia.

137. The three types of muscular tissue are
a. origin, insertion, and belly.
b. striated, nonstriated, and cardiac.
c. anterior, posterior, and frontalis.
d. supinator, pronator, and flexor.

Facials

138. After analyzing the client's skin, the first step in a facial is
a. applying cleansing cream.
b. removing makeup.
c. steaming the client's face.
d. applying massage cream.

139. When removing cleansing cream, you would start at the client's
  a. back.
  b. chest.
  c. neck.
  d. forehead.

140. For a client with oily skin, press out blackheads immediately after
  a. cleansing the face.
  b. massaging the face.
  c. steaming the face.
  d. applying an astringent lotion.

141. The purpose of using infrared rays or electric current during a facial is to
  a. deep cleanse the skin.
  b. increase the cost to the client.
  c. use expensive equipment.
  d. help lotion penetrate the skin.

142. Which statement about the diet for a client with acne is correct?
  a. Acne is caused by specific food allergies; the client should have allergy testing.
  b. The client should consult with a doctor about an appropriate diet.
  c. You can safely tell the client to eliminate all fats and salt from the diet.
  d. The client should avoid chocolate, nuts, and red wine, and limit fluid intake.

143. A cosmetologist who specializes in skin care is called
  a. a cosmetician.
  b. an esthetician.
  c. a makeup artist.
  d. a colorist.

144. Which of the following is **NOT** a common reason that clients give for dissatisfaction with facials?
  a. The cosmetologist does not present herself professionally.
  b. The cosmetologist does not treat the client respectfully.
  c. The cosmetologist does not follow correct sanitary procedures.
  d. The cosmetologist is extremely organized and has all materials on hand.

145. For which skin type are pack facials recommended?
  a. dry skin
  b. oily skin
  c. all skin types
  d. aging skin

146. What skin types are hydrating masks recommended for?
  a. combination skin
  b. oily skin
  c. dry and mature skin
  d. blemished skin

Facial Makeup

147. In general, eye shadow that is darker than the client's iris will make her eyes appear
  a. darker.
  b. lighter.
  c. bluer.
  d. greener.

148. Your client has a very round face. Where should you apply corrective makeup?
  a. down the sides of the face
  b. on the cheekbones
  c. on the nose and chin
  d. at the top and bottom of the face

149. To correct a broad nose, you should use a darker shade of foundation
   a. on the sides of the nose.
   b. above the nose.
   c. below the nose.
   d. down the sides of the face.

150. You can use makeup to make very round eyes look wider by
   a. shading the inner corner most heavily.
   b. extending the shadow in close to the nose.
   c. using very light shadow under the brows and in the crease.
   d. extending the shadow past the outer corner of the eye.

151. The most natural and attractive shape of the eyebrows is
   a. an arch that follows the curved shape of the eye socket.
   b. an arch just below the curve of the eye socket.
   c. a straight line that follows the top of the eye socket.
   d. a straight line just below the top of the eye socket.

152. It is necessary to do an allergy test before
   a. doing facial makeup.
   b. arching eyebrows.
   c. applying artificial eyelash strips.
   d. applying semipermanent individual eyelashes.

153. After they are used for facial makeup, all washable linens, such as towels and capes, should be placed
   a. on the floor for laundry collection.
   b. in a drawer for reuse.
   c. in a closed laundry receptacle.
   d. immediately in the washing machine.

Hair Removal

154. Which statement about use of hot wax to remove hair is correct?
   a. The wax is applied in the opposite direction of hair growth.
   b. It is safe if hot wax gets into the client's eyes.
   c. The wax is removed in the opposite direction of hair growth.
   d. The wax is removed slowly and gently.

155. A skin sensitivity test is necessary before using
   a. a hot wax depilatory.
   b. a cold wax depilatory.
   c. electronic tweezers.
   d. a chemical depilatory.

156. Which of the following is a permanent method of hair removal?
   a. waxing
   b. lasering
   c. sugaring
   d. epilating

157. To perform laser hair removal, you need to have
   a. no special training.
   b. specialized training.
   c. an additional license.
   d. a certification.

158. The removal of hair by means of an electric current that destroys the root of the hair is called
   a. electrolysis.
   b. electrology.
   c. photo depilation.
   d. laser epilating.

159. Which of the following can perform electrolysis?
a. a licensed electrician
b. a licensed esthetician
c. a licensed electrologist
d. a licensed cosmetologist

160. When is waxing a method of permanent hair removal?
a. when the hair is coarse
b. never
c. when the hair is fine
d. always

▶ Chemical Services

Permanent Waving

161. Porosity refers to the hair's ability to
a. retain its curl.
b. hold a shape.
c. resist moisture.
d. absorb liquid.

162. The processing time used for the waving lotion depends on the hair's
a. porosity and texture.
b. texture and elasticity.
c. elasticity and density.
d. density and length.

163. To perm hair that is longer than six inches, you should use
a. an alkaline-based waving lotion.
b. an extra-long waving time.
c. small partings.
d. large rods.

164. The dropped-crown wrapping pattern is used for a style with
a. tight curls all over.
b. tight curls at the crown only.
c. a smooth crown.
d. bangs.

165. The purpose of a preliminary test curl is to determine
a. how much to charge for the perm.
b. whether the client will want a facial after the perm.
c. whether the client will like the finished hairstyle.
d. how the client's hair will react to the perm.

166. It is advisable to take a preliminary test curl on hair that is
a. normally porous.
b. naturally curly.
c. damaged or tinted.
d. very long.

167. You should apply waving lotion to the
a. top and bottom of each rod.
b. top of each rod only.
c. area between the rods.
d. client's top hairline and allow it to drip down slowly.

168. Right after rinsing the waving lotion from the hair, the next step is to
a. apply the neutralizer.
b. blot off excess water.
c. blow dry the hair.
d. set and style the hair.

169. Naturally curly hair with an uneven curl pattern can usually be successfully permed with
a. a body wave.
b. very narrow rods.
c. an alkaline waving lotion.
d. heated clamps.

170. When perming hair that has been tinted, bleached, or highlighted, you should use a product that
a. is strongly alkaline.
b. remains on the hair a very short time.
c. includes a pre-wrap lotion.
d. works with heat.

Hair Coloring

171. When used to describe a color, the word tone refers to
a. darkness.
b. porosity.
c. density.
d. warmth.

172. Which of the following is a secondary color?
a. pink
b. orange
c. teal
d. brown

173. Which of the following is NOT a tertiary color?
a. blue-green
b. red-violet
c. yellow
d. yellow-orange

174. What effect do complementary colors have on each other?
a. they develop each other
b. they brighten each other
c. they darken each other
d. they neutralize each other

175. When applying a temporary color rinse, you should wear gloves because
a. these products can stain the skin as well as the hair.
b. these products are highly toxic to the skin and eyes.
c. this avoids the spread of infection.
d. most people are allergic to these products.

176. Because semipermanent hair coloring products do not change the structure of the hair shaft, they are often used on clients who have
a. fine or damaged hair.
b. allergies to most hair coloring products.
c. very dark hair.
d. coarse or very curly hair.

177. Permanent hair colors differ from temporary hair colors because they
a. both lighten and deposit color.
b. can only darken the hair.
c. cannot cause damage to fine hair.
d. can be used on previously-tinted hair.

178. Hydrogen peroxide bleaches the color out of hair by
a. diluting the melanin globules and making them appear lighter.
b. allowing melanin to combine with oxygen and diffuse through the hair shaft.
c. coating the hair so that melanin cannot enter the cuticle layer.
d. acting as a solvent and diluting the solution of melanin and protein.

179. The advantage of single-process tints is that they can simultaneously
a. lighten the hair and add color.
b. darken and condition the hair.
c. cleanse and condition the hair.
d. lighten the hair and remove color.

180. To a colorist, the term lift refers to
a. color highlights.
b. natural sheen.
c. lightening action.
d. color matching.

181. Fading is a particular problem on hair that is tinted
a. red.
b. blonde.
c. dark brown.
d. black.

182. Your client's hair is tinted a medium red-brown, but she now requests a change to a lighter shade. It will be necessary for you to first
a. select a complementary tint.
b. add a filler tint.
c. recondition her hair before adding a semipermanent rinse.
d. remove the present tint.

183. Adding a lighter color in small, carefully selected areas is known as
a. backlighting.
b. tipping.
c. highlighting.
d. decolorizing.

184. A penetrating hair color is one that
a. washes out after approximately eight shampoos.
b. enters the cortex of the hair shaft.
c. is not mixed with a developer.
d. is not alkaline.

185. Melanin pigment is naturally present throughout the hair's
a. cuticle.
b. medulla.
c. cortex.
d. papilla.

186. When you add pigment to fine hair, the effect will be especially dark because
a. the melanin granules are grouped closely together.
b. there are more hairs per square inch.
c. fine hair contains more melanin than other types of hair.
d. fine hair contains more melanin granules than other types.

187. Before the client decides on a color service, it is important that you carefully explain
a. the process, cost, and upkeep involved.
b. the chemical process involved.
c. that you can guarantee that you will achieve a specific shade.
d. that hair coloring carries the risk of allergic reaction.

188. When should a patch test be given?
a. 24 to 48 seconds prior to application.
b. 24 to 48 minutes prior to application.
c. 24 to 48 hours prior to application.
d. 24 to 48 days prior to application.

189. You should choose a warm hair color for a client with which type of skin tone?
a. olive
b. red
c. neutral
d. golden

190. Green tones in a hair color usually result from
   a. too much red in the mix.
   b. reaction to a chemical, such as chlorine.
   c. hair that is not sufficiently porous.
   d. not enough orange in the mix.

191. Your client complains that her hair color is "too red." You determine that her hair is actually a level 7 orange. To neutralize the brassy tones, you should select a
   a. level 7 green.
   b. level 8 green.
   c. level 7 blue.
   d. level 8 blue.

192. Hydrogen peroxide should be stored in a
   a. clear glass bottle in the refrigerator.
   b. plastic container in a warm place.
   c. opaque container in a cool, dark place.
   d. clear glass container in direct sunlight.

193. Your formula calls for 10 ounces of 20-volume hydrogen peroxide. You have 2 ounces of 100-volume hydrogen peroxide. How much water should you add to achieve the desired concentration?
   a. 2 ounces
   b. 4 ounces
   c. 6 ounces
   d. 8 ounces

194. A very pale blond color can be safely achieved by
   a. one prolonged application of bleach.
   b. using a combination of semipermanent and permanent hair colors.
   c. lightening to pale yellow and then using a toner.
   d. up to three applications of bleach.

195. If a test strand comes out too dark, you should either
   a. increase the strength of the lightener or increase the processing time.
   b. increase the strength of the mixture or decrease the processing time.
   c. decrease the strength of the mixture or increase the processing time.
   d. decrease the strength of the mixture or decrease the processing time.

196. You remove a toner by
   a. applying hydrogen peroxide to neutralize it.
   b. shampooing twice.
   c. brushing the hair vigorously.
   d. wetting the hair and massaging it to a lather.

197. A color additive is
   a. a hair color product.
   b. a semipermanent hair color.
   c. a particular combination of dyes that make up a specific hair color.
   d. a concentrated color used to intensify or tone down a hair color.

Chemical Hair Relaxing

198. During a relaxer test, the test strand of hair breaks. You should
   a. refuse to treat the client's hair.
   b. condition the client's hair.
   c. do another test with a weaker solution.
   d. recommend thermal hair relaxing to the client.

199. When you chemically relax a client's hair with a "no base" relaxer, always
   a. protect the entire scalp with a petroleum cream.
   b. apply a protective cream to the hairline and ears.
   c. make sure the hair is wet before beginning the procedure.
   d. part the hair into no more than three sections.

200. When retouching a client's hair with a sodium hydroxide relaxer, you should
   a. relax the entire head again.
   b. relax only the curliest parts of the hair.
   c. wait at least six months between treatments.
   d. relax the new growth only.

201. A chemical hair relaxer that is formulated for fine, color-treated, or damaged hair would be labeled as what strength?
   a. low strength
   b. mild strength
   c. regular strength
   d. super strength

202. Relaxers with ammonium thioglycolate differ from relaxers with sodium hydroxide because thio relaxers are
   a. milder.
   b. quicker.
   c. more dangerous.
   d. hotter.

203. When giving a soft curl perm, you should take a test curl frequently in order to ensure that the
   a. hair is not becoming more curly.
   b. hair is curling properly but not becoming damaged.
   c. client's skin is not becoming irritated.
   d. heat is not too great for the client to stand.

204. Which statement about chemically relaxed hair is correct?
   a. You should not use a thio relaxer on hair previously treated with sodium hydroxide.
   b. You should not use heat of any kind on chemically relaxed hair.
   c. A protective base is always needed for a sodium hydroxide relaxer.
   d. Never use sodium hydroxide on very fine hair.

▶ Hair Design

Haircutting

205. In the five-section parting method, section 1 is located
   a. from the forehead to the crown.
   b. at the back of the head.
   c. above the right ear.
   d. above the left ear.

206. When holding haircutting scissors, you place your thumb
   a. on the finger brace.
   b. in the ring of the movable blade.
   c. in the ring of the still blade.
   d. on the pivot.

207. The terms slithering and effiliating refer to the process of
   a. cutting tinted hair.
   b. cutting very curly hair.
   c. thinning the hair.
   d. finger waving the hair.

208. After dividing the hair into sections, the next step in haircutting is to
a. cut the hair in section 1.
b. blunt cut sections 2 and 3.
c. divide section 5 into two equal parts and blunt cut.
d. decide on the length of the nape guideline hair.

209. To cut bangs, you should position yourself
a. in front of the client.
b. in back of the client.
c. on a low stool.
d. above the top of the client's head.

210. The guide for cutting each section of hair is the
a. nape hair.
b. height of the earlobe.
c. previously cut section.
d. crown hair.

211. A technique for creating fullness in a haircut by cutting the ends of the hair at a slight taper is called
a. razoring.
b. beveling.
c. texturing.
d. slithering.

212. In a blunt or one-length haircut, what degree of elevation is employed?
a. 90
b. 45
c. 30
d. 0

213. Which of the following is NOT a reason for using reference points in haircutting?
a. to ensure balance within the design
b. to allow for the recreation of the same haircut again
c. to indicate where and when to change technique to compensate for irregularities in the head form
d. to determine the length the hair should be cut to

214. The area of the head between the apex and the back of the parietal ridge is called the
a. occipital bone.
b. crown.
c. top of the head.
d. sides of the head.

215. What do layers in a hair cut create?
a. weight
b. texture
c. movement
d. tension

216. When cutting curly hair it is important to remember that it will
a. extend much more after it dries than straight hair.
b. change color much more after it dries than straight hair.
c. shrink much more after it dries than straight hair.
d. straighten much more after it dries than straight hair.

217. The clipper is used to
a. make the first guide cut.
b. finish off the crown hair.
c. trim the neck hair.
d. thin the hair.

Hair Styling

218. In finger waving, which statement about forming the first ridge is correct?
  a. Emphasize the ridge by pushing it outward with your fingers.
  b. The first ridge begins at the crown of the head.
  c. The first ridge is formed by inserting the comb beneath your index finger and pulling forward.
  d. With the teeth of the comb still inserted in the first ridge, you would next pull the hair away from the head.

219. The second ridge begins at the
  a. level of the earlobe.
  b. hairline level.
  c. nape of the neck.
  d. crown of the head.

220. Which statement about bases for pin curls is **INCORRECT**?
  a. The finished curl is affected by the shape of the base.
  b. Square base curls should be staggered in a brick-laying format.
  c. Triangular base curls are used along the facial hairline.
  d. You subdivide sections of hair into bases for pincurls.

221. When shaping waved bangs with pin curls, what is the relationship between hair texture and number of pin curls?
  a. The finer the hair, the more pin curls.
  b. Normal hair should have exactly one pin curl per square inch.
  c. The coarser the hair, the more pin curls.
  d. There is no relationship.

222. After removing the rollers and clips from a setting, the next step is to
  a. wet down the hair slightly.
  b. apply setting lotion.
  c. thoroughly brush the hair.
  d. back comb the back hair.

223. Back combing is used to.
  a. remove tangles from hair.
  b. add volume to a hairstyle.
  c. hide the roots of tinted hair.
  d. smooth out curl patterns.

224. A client with close-set eyes should have a hairstyle that is
  a. asymmetrical.
  b. swept back.
  c. wide at the bottom.
  d. wide at the top.

225. For a client with a long, thin neck, the hair should
  a. be upswept and full on top.
  b. fall in long, full waves.
  c. be asymmetrical.
  d. be very full around the face.

226. For a client with a protruding chin, you should create a hairstyle with fullness at the
  a. chin level
  b. crown of the head
  c. forehead
  d. nape of the neck

227. Practice with using thermal irons is intended to help you develop
  a. an impressive repertoire of moves.
  b. a smooth, rotating motion.
  c. strength in your grip.
  d. resistance to injury from heat.

228. After heating and rolling a full-base curl, place it
a. forward and high on its base.
b. in the center of its base.
c. half-way off its base.
d. completely off its base.

229. When using curling irons, you should NOT use a comb that is made of
a. metal or celluloid.
b. hard rubber.
c. heat-proof plastic.
d. nonflammable material.

230. When blow-drying hair, using a large-diameter brush results in
a. loose curls.
b. curly hair.
c. a long-lasting hairstyle.
d. a layered hairstyle.

231. When styling a client's hair with an air waver, it is most important to
a. follow the hair's natural waves.
b. have the hair completely dry first.
c. use a large-diameter brush.
d. cut the hair with blunt ends.

232. To make sure that a blown-dry hairstyle holds in place, it is most important to
a. have the hair cut with blunt ends.
b. get the hair and scalp completely dry.
c. use the largest brush available.
d. use the hottest drying temperature the client can stand.

Thermal Hair Straightening

233. The rule for deciding on the size of the subsections to use when pressing hair is
a. the finer the hair, the larger the sections.
b. the finer the hair, the smaller the sections.
c. the curlier the hair, the larger the sections.
d. the curlier the hair, the smaller the sections.

234. You should control the heat carefully when pressing lightened or tinted hair because it is more likely to
a. frizz.
b. curl up.
c. discolor.
d. coarsen.

235. Very short hair presents particular problems in pressing because of the possibility that the
a. iron will burn the client.
b. hair will frizz or curl.
c. hair will fall out at the roots.
d. iron will not be hot enough.

236. How much curl does a hard press remove?
a. 40–50%
b. 60–74%
c. 75%
d. 100%

237. In the event of a scalp burn you should immediately
a. re-shampoo the client's hair.
b. apply 1% gentian violet jelly.
c. apply cotton balls dipped in ice water.
d. wet the area that has been burned with cold water, then apply a light dusting of talcum powder to absorb the heat.

COSMETOLOGY REFRESHER COURSE

Braiding and Extensions

238. When braiding or weaving hair it is best if the hair is
a. dry.
b. semi-dry.
c. semi-wet.
d. wet.

239. A three-strand braid that employs the underhand technique, in which strands of hair are woven under the center strand is called:
a. an invisible braid.
b. an indivisible braid.
c. a visible braid.
d. a visual braid.

240. A man or a woman who wears narrow rows of visible braids that lie close to the scalp is wearing what type of braid?
a. visible
b. cornrow
c. underhand
d. invisible

241. Natural textured hair that is intertwined and meshed together to form a single or separate network of hair describes
a. hair locking.
b. hair stepping.
c. hair meshing.
d. hair winding.

242. If a bulb can be felt at the end of each lock, the hair begins to regain length and the locks are closed at the ends, dense and dull, not reflecting any light, what stage of maturation is the lock in?
a. pre-lock stage
b. sprouting stage
c. growing stage
d. maturation stage

243. To remove bonded wefts from the hair, you must soak them in
a. acetone.
b. warm water.
c. oil.
d. cool water.

244. What method of attachment is best for clients with fine, limp hair?
a. sew and cut method
b. bonding method
c. track and sew method
d. fusion method

245. What aspect of the track determines how the hair will fall?
a. reference
b. angle
c. length
d. cut

Wigs and Hair Enhancements

246. When ordering a wig for a client, you should specify the measurements, hair color, type of hair, length of hair, and
a. finished style.
b. hair parting and pattern.
c. client's eye color.
d. client's skin color.

247. You can stretch a wig that is too small by
a. wetting it, pinning it to a larger size block, and putting it under a hot dryer.
b. cutting it apart and resewing it.
c. wetting it, pinning it to a larger size block, and letting it dry naturally.
d. wetting it and letting it dry on the client's head.

248. When you cut and shape a wig, the best way to ensure that the style will suit the client's features is to
   a. use a picture of the client as a guide.
   b. cut it while it is on the client.
   c. cut it to the client's directions.
   d. use a picture of a model the client thinks is attractive.

249. Which statement about cutting a synthetic wig is correct?
   a. Cut the wig while dry, using scissors and thinning shears.
   b. Cut the wig while dry, using a razor.
   c. Cut the wig while wet, using scissors and thinning shears.
   d. Cut the wig while wet, using a razor.

250. When combing out a newly set wig, use a
   a. narrow-tooth comb.
   b. wide-tooth comb.
   c. natural bristle brush.
   d. wire bristle brush.

▶ Answers

Scientific and Basic Concepts

Life Skills

1. **c.** Properly conducting your interactions with your employer, clients, and your coworkers is an example of professional ethics.

2. **b.** A mission statement sets forth the values that an individual or institution lives by and establishes future goals.

3. **d.** Professional ethics involves practicing the highest standards of sanitation at all times.

4. **d.** The four basic styles of learning are: interactive, systematic, intuitive, and reader/listener.

5. **c.** Procrastination is the act of putting off until tomorrow what you can do today.

Your Professional Image

6. **d.** A balanced diet should include a variety of different foods.

7. **d.** Regular exercise is one of the most important things you can do to help maintain good health.

8. **c.** The most basic rule of personal hygiene is to take a daily bath or shower. Good posture (answer **d**), while an important part of general health, is not part of hygiene per se.

9. **a.** Good posture means standing with the back straight.

10. **b.** A positive approach, including pleasant, gracious manners, is part of a professional attitude toward clients.

11. **b.** Rest your body weight on the full length of your thighs while sitting to avoid constricting one specific area.

Communicating For Success

12. **a.** Do not display anger toward a difficult client. Remain calm, and try to determine what the specific problem is by asking open-ended questions.

13. **d.** Communication is the act of transmitting information, in the form of symbols, gestures, or behaviors, in order to express an idea or concept so that it is satisfactorily understood.

14. **c.** Before consulting with a client, a good communicator should collect his or her thoughts and feelings and be sure he or she knows what he or she wants to communicate.

15. **c.** Articulation occurs whenever someone clearly expresses their thoughts, feelings, and desires.

16. **c.** When you clarify the message you make it clear by eliminating distractions.

17. **c.** A consultation should be part of every single service and salon visit.

18. **b.** Only take a tardy client if you determine that you can service the client without jeopardizing another client's appointment.

19. **b.** Leaving messages is **NOT** one of the three basic processes of communicating.

20. **b.** Translating your thoughts and feelings into symbols that can be easily understood by others is the second step in the communications process.

Bacteriology

21. **c.** The body's main defenses against infection are unbroken skin, white blood cells, body secretions such as digestive juices, and antitoxins. Red blood cells have other functions within the body.

22. **a.** A carrier is someone who can transmit a disease to others without being sick himself or herself.

23. **a.** Ringworm is a fungus infection of the skin.

24. **a.** AIDS can be spread only by the sharing of blood or other body fluids. For example, if you accidentally cut a person with AIDS and get blood on your scissors, the virus could be spread to another person unless the scissors are properly sterilized.

25. a. The most common pus-forming bacteria are staphylococci.

26. c. Cosmetologists should **NOT** treat skin diseases; instead, you should refer the client to a physician.

27. a. Nonpathogenic organisms are helpful and they perform many useful functions, such as decomposing garbage.

28. d. Spirilla bacteria are shaped like corkscrews.

29. b. Cocci bacteria move through the air.

Decontamination and Infection Control

30. a. Disinfectants are used to kill microorganisms on nonliving surfaces only. They should never be used on human skin, hair, or nails.

31. b. Because disinfectants are such strong chemicals, you should always follow the manufacturers' directions when using them.

32. b. Always clean instruments thoroughly before placing them in disinfectant solution.

33. a. Quat is short for quaternary ammonium compound, an effective and safe disinfectant.

34. a. Always wear rubber gloves and goggles when handling powerful chemicals such as disinfectants in order to protect your hands and eyes.

35. c. Sanitation means keeping every item and surface in the salon clean and properly disinfected.

36. d. It is important to use the proper procedure in disinfecting a countertop. The incomplete procedures listed in the other answer choices are likely to leave potentially harmful materials on the countertop surface.

37. d. Ethyl alcohol must be used in a solution no weaker than 70% to be an effective disinfectant.

38. c. The solution used in a wet sanitizer should be changed every day.

Properties of the Hair and Scalp

39. c. The health of a person's hair is most influenced by the person's physical and emotional health.

40. a. A cowlick is a tuft of hair that stands straight up.

41. a. The cuticle is the outermost protective layer of the hair shaft.

42. c. The purpose of scalp manipulation (scalp massage) is to relax the client and to stimulate blood circulation in the scalp.

43. a. Oil treatments are beneficial for split ends. The other treatments mentioned would not help and might aggravate the problem.

44. d. A boil, or furuncle, is an acute, painful infection of a hair follicle.

45. b. Clients with head lice should never be treated in the salon, since head lice spread so easily. The other choices are correct statements about head lice.

46. d. The bulb of the hair fits around and over the papilla at the base of the hair shaft.

47. a. The shape and direction of the follicle determines the direction of hair growth.

48. c. The average person sheds approximately 40–100 hairs per day.

49. b. The three hair shapes are round, almost flat, and oval.

The Nail and Its Disorders

50. b. A normal, healthy nail grows forward, starting at the matrix and extending over the tip of the finger.

51. a. Younger persons' nails grow more quickly than those of older people. The other statements are incorrect.

52. b. A nail that is lost because of disease will probably grow back distorted.

53. c. If a client is accidentally cut during a manicure, apply antiseptic and a sterile bandage to help prevent infection. The other answer choices are overreactions to a minor injury.

54. b. A nail disorder is a condition caused by injury to the nail or some disease or imbalance in the body.

55. c. A fungus infection in the nail most commonly appears as a discoloration that spreads toward the cuticle.

56. a. Manicure a hypertrophied nail as long as no infection is present. Of course, if an infection is present, you should refer the client to a physician.

The Skin and Its Disorders

57. d. The sweat glands regulate body temperature (primarily by helping to cool the body) and secrete waste products.

58. d. The main functions of the skin include protection, sensation, heat regulation, excretion, and secretion of sebum. Digestion is a function of the digestive system.

59. a. Chronic inflammation of the sebaceous glands is the definition of acne, which can occur anywhere on the body.

60. a. Dermatitis refers to any inflammation of the skin, no matter what the cause.

61. c. You should not remove hair from a mole.

62. d. In addition to its use in acne treatment, Retin-A is also used to prevent or slow down the development of wrinkles.

63. c. The skin is the thickest on the palms and the soles.

64. d. Subcutaneous tissue is located below the dermis (note: the suffix *sub* means *below*).

Cells, Anatomy, and Physiology

65. c. The skeleton supports and protects the internal organs. Specialized cells within the long bones also produce blood cells.

66. b. The lower jawbone is called the mandible.

67. a. The frontalis muscle controls the movement of the forehead.

68. d. The muscles surrounding the ear have almost no function.

69. a. The vascular system, which circulates blood throughout the body, consists of the heart and blood vessels.

70. c. The capillaries nourish the individual body cells.

71. c. The skin's function as an excretory organ is to perspire, which rids the body of waste products.

72. d. A person's rate of breathing, rather than staying the same all the time, increases with increased activity.

Electricity and Light Therapy

73. c. The 2 types of electric current are direct current which is a constant, even-flowing current that travels in one direction only and produces a chemical reaction; and alternating current which is a rapid and interrupted current, flowing first in one direction and then in the opposite direction.

74. d. The primary source of lights used for facial and scalp treatments are visible light rays.

75. c. The benefit of white light is that it has the benefits of all the rays of the visible spectrum.

76. a. The positive electrode is effective in closing enlarged pores.

77. c. The Tesla current works by producing heat (it is thermal), and it is also germicidal.

78. c. The ultraviolet lamp is usually placed about 36 inches from the skin surface.

79. d. The drying effects of ultraviolet rays are beneficial to conditions such as acne and seborrhea.

80. d. Electricity is a form of energy that, when in motion, exhibits magnetic, chemical, or thermal effects. It is a flow of electrons, which are negatively charged subatomic particles.

81. **b.** An electric current is the flow of electricity along a conductor, an element that transmits electricity.

82. **c.** A complete circuit is the path of an electric current from the generating source through conductors and back to its original source.

Chemistry

83. **d.** A neutral pH reading—that is, an indication that a substance is neither acid nor alkaline— is 7.

84. **a.** Anionics are the most commonly used detergents, or surfactants.

85. **d.** Sodium hydroxide, which has a pH of 13, is strongly alkaline. It is a caustic chemical that must be handled with extreme caution.

86. **a.** Because of the large molecular weight of the pigment molecules, temporary hair colors cannot enter into the hair shaft but rather remain on the surface.

87. **b.** Cleansing cream is a water-in-oil emulsion. The other choices are examples of oil-in-water solutions.

88. **c.** Ethyl methacrylate is a chemical compound used in many sculptured nails.

89. **a.** An element cannot be separated into a simpler substance by ordinary chemical means.

90. **a.** Polymers are chemicals that form long chains and thus coat the hair shafts and hold them in place.

The Salon Business

91. **b.** Permission to renovate a property is usually obtained from the local (town or city) government.

92. **d.** In most states, both the state and federal governments levy income taxes.

93. **d.** The business owner usually has the most control over advertising costs, which the owner can increase or decrease whenever he or she wants. Rent, supplies, and salaries are costs over which the owner has less control.

94. **c.** A business plan is most like a map in that it lays out all of the options you might take and helps you to chart the best route to your final goals.

95. **c.** The business plan includes every aspect of the business, but not how individuals will use the profits of their business unless it is to be reinvested in the business.

96. **a.** Careful inventory records will help you reorder in time so you do not miss potential sales.

97. **b.** The size of your salon will determine the number of staffers you will need to hire to achieve maximum efficiency and productivity of the salon space.

98. **c.** Poor or ineffective managers are reluctant to share information with staff because they are afraid of losing power.

99. **d.** Be courteous, identify yourself, and ask what you can do for the client. On the other hand, don't go overboard with a long greeting that may make the client impatient.

100. **a.** Always listen courteously to everything the client has to say before suggesting a solution.

101. **a.** Always consider the client's best interest. Providing good service will increase business in the long run.

102. **b.** A salon typically spends about 3% of its gross income on advertising.

Physical Services

Draping

103. **c.** Make sure that the cape does not touch the client's skin, where it can cause discomfort to the client.

104. **a.** Careful draping is important because it shows consideration for the client's comfort.

105. **a.** Wrap a towel over the client's shoulders, then the cape, and then another towel.

106. **d.** The neck strip should prevent any part of the cape from touching the client's skin.

107. c. To protect your client's clothing have the client change into a gown and use a waterproof shampoo cape before beginning the service.

108. b. Have the client remove earrings, necklaces, and any other jewelry or adornment around the face, neck and head.

Shampooing, Rinsing, and Conditioning

109. c. Never brush a client's hair if the scalp is irritated.

110. b. Monitor the water temperature continuously while shampooing to make sure it doesn't get uncomfortably hot or cold.

111. c. Support the client's head in your left hand while you manipulate the scalp with your right.

112. d. Squeeze the hair to remove excess lather before rinsing.

113. b. Have the client rinse the shampoo from her eye immediately to avoid additional irritation.

114. d. Protein is a conditioning agent.

115. d. Medicated shampoos are more expensive than other shampoos, but they are effective when prescribed by a physician to treat specific scalp conditions, such as problem dandruff.

116. b. Acid-balanced rinses are used to preserve the color of tinted hair and keep it from fading.

Manicuring and Pedicuring

117. c. Clean the manicure table with a disinfectant before each manicure in order to kill any potentially harmful bacteria.

118. a. Apply a mild antiseptic to the cut to help prevent infection.

119. c. Always remove the cuticle as a single piece.

120. c. The hand massage is done after the nail preparation and before applying nail polish.

121. b. Massage the calf muscles, moving toward the heart. You should not massage the shinbone or above the knee.

122. a. Do not treat corns, calluses, or ingrown toenails—that's a physician's job, not a cosmetologist's.

Advanced Nail Techniques

123. a. Roughing up the nail surface allows the wrap to adhere to it.

124. b. Sculptured nails are also known as built-on nails, since the nail extension is built on an existing foundation.

125. c. Artificial nails should not be immersed in water for very long.

126. d. Select a nail tip that fits the tip of the client's nail, and shape as needed.

127. b. A nail tip should never cover more than one-half of the natural nail plate.

128. a. Nail antiseptic must be applied to the natural nail before applying the nail tip to remove the remaining natural oil and to dehydrate the nail for better adhesion.

129. d. To remove nail tips, first remove any polish and place the client's fingertips in a bowl with enough acetone to cover the nails and soak them for the amount of time recommended by the manufacturer, then use a fresh orangewood stick or a metal pusher to slide off the softened tips.

130. a. A liquid nail wrap is a polish made with tiny fibers designed to strengthen and preserve the natural nail as it grows.

131. d. Acrylic nails, often referred to as sculptured nails, are artificial nails that are created by combining a liquid acrylic product with a powdered product.

132. a. A primer is a substance that improves adhesion, or attachment, and prepares the nail surface for bonding with the acrylic material.

Theory of Massage

133. a. Petrissage is a kneading movement.

134. d. Percussion, which consists of tapping or slapping movements, is the most stimulating type of massage.

135. a. Use light finger taps only to the face to avoid causing discomfort to the client and damaging sensitive tissues.

136. b. Do not massage a client who has heart disease, circulatory disease, or high blood pressure. You may provide a massage to clients with the other listed conditions if you follow appropriate precautions.

137. b. The three types of muscular tissue are striated (also called skeletal or voluntary muscles), nonstriated (also called involuntary, visceral, or smooth muscles), and cardiac (the heart).

Facials

138. a. Deep cleansing, which begins with the application of cleansing cream, is the first major step in a facial.

139. d. When removing cleansing cream, start at the forehead.

140. c. Remove blackheads with gentle pressure immediately after steaming the face, when the pores are open.

141. d. Heat and electric current stimulate the skin and help lotions and creams penetrate better.

142. b. Have the client consult with a physician about an appropriate diet.

143. b. An esthetician specializes in skin care.

144. d. The cosmetologist should be organized and have all materials readily available; the other choices are things the cosmetologist should not do.

145. c. Pack facials are recommended for all skin types and are usually applied directly to the skin.

146. c. Hydrating masks are recommended for dry and mature skin or skin that appears lifeless

and dull. Gauze is often used to aid in holding the mask preparation on the face.

Facial Makeup

147. b. A darker eye shadow will generally make the eyes appear to be lighter.

148. a. Apply corrective makeup down the sides of the face for a client with a round face.

149. a. Blending a darker shade of foundation down the sides of the nose will minimize its width.

150. d. Extending the shadow out past the outer corner of the eye will make the eyes look wider.

151. a. Shape the eyebrow so that the curve follows the top of the eye socket.

152. d. An allergy test is necessary because of the adhesive used in semipermanent eyelashes.

153. c. For sanitary reasons, place used linens in a closed laundry receptacle immediately.

Hair Removal

154. c. Remove the wax quickly, in the opposite direction of hair growth.

155. d. A skin test is necessary before using a chemical depilatory.

156. b. Laser hair removal is a permanent form of hair removal.

157. b. In certain states and provinces, cosmetologists or estheticians are allowed to perform laser hair removal. This method requires specialized training, most commonly offered by laser equipment manufacturers.

158. a. The removal of hair by means of an electric current that destroys the root of the hair is called electrolysis.

159. c. Only a licensed electrologist may perform electrolysis.

160. b. Electrolysis, photo-epilation, and laser hair removal are the only forms of permanent hair removal.

Chemical Services

Permanent Waving

161. d. Porosity refers to the ability to absorb liquid.

162. a. Processing time depends on the hair's porosity and texture.

163. c. To permanently wave longer hair, use small partings to allow the chemicals to penetrate.

164. c. The dropped-crown wrap is used for styles with a smooth crown.

165. d. The purpose of a test curl is to determine how the client's hair will react.

166. c. A preliminary test curl is especially advisable on hair that is damaged or tinted.

167. a. Apply waving lotion to the top and underside of each wound rod.

168. b. After rinsing, the next step is to blot excess water before applying neutralizer.

169. a. A body wave will even out curly hair and make it more manageable.

170. c. For tinted, bleached, or highlighted hair, choose a product with a pre-wrap lotion that can fill in the porous areas of the hair.

Hair Coloring

171. d. The term tone refers to the warmth or coolness of a color.

172. b. A secondary color is a color obtained by mixing equal parts of two primary colors. The secondary colors are: green, orange, and violet.

173. c. A tertiary color is an intermediate color achieved by mixing a secondary color and its neighboring primary color on the color wheel in equal amounts. The tertiary colors include: blue-green, blue-violet, red-violet, red-orange, yellow-orange, and yellow-green.

174. d. Because they are opposite on the color wheel, complementary colors neutralize each other.

175. a. Temporary rinses can stain the skin as well as the hair.

176. a. Semipermanent hair coloring products are often used on clients with very fine or previously damaged hair.

177. a. Because permanent products both lighten and apply color, a wide range of effects are possible with these products.

178. b. Hydrogen peroxide is an oxidizer, a substance that allows oxygen to combine with another substance.

179. a. Single-process tints both lighten and add color in one step.

180. c. The term lift refers to a product's lightening action, that is, its ability to remove the natural hair color.

181. a. Fading is a particular problem with red tints.

182. d. It is necessary to remove the present, darker tint before adding a lighter one.

183. c. Adding color in selected areas is highlighting.

184. b. A penetrating color is one that enters the cortex of the hair shaft.

185. c. Melanin pigment is scattered throughout the cortex of each hair.

186. a. In fine hair, the melanin granules are grouped more closely together, so the effect is of a darker color.

187. a. Make sure that the client understands all these factors, presented in a positive light, before making a decision.

188. c. The patch test must be given 24 to 48 hours prior to application, you must use the exact same type of color as will be used for the haircolor service, and the tint should remain undisturbed on the test site for 24 hours.

189. d. Warm hair colors are recommended for clients with golden skin tones.

190. b. Greenish tones most often result from reaction to a chemical in the environment, such as chlorine in a swimming pool.

191. d. Neutralize an unwanted color with a complementary color that is a shade darker; in this case, level 8 blue will neutralize a level 7 orange.

192. c. Both heat and light cause hydrogen peroxide to break down.

193. d. Two ounces of 100-volume hydrogen peroxide plus 8 ounces of water will result in 10 ounces of 20-volume hydrogen peroxide.

194. c. Lightening to pale yellow and then using a toner is the safe way to achieve a very light blond color.

195. a. If a test strand is not sufficiently lightened, you need to increase either the strength of the lightener or the processing time.

196. d. Remove the toner by wetting the hair and massaging it until it lathers.

197. d. This is the correct definition of a color additive, which is also called a color concentrate.

Chemical Hair Relaxing

198. c. Part of the point of doing a test strand is to see how the client's hair will tolerate the treatment. If the test strand breaks, do another test using a milder solution.

199. b. When using a "no base" product, apply a protective cream to the client's hairline and ears only.

200. d. Relax the new growth only during a retouch.

201. b. A mild chemical hair relaxer is one that is formulated for fine, color-treated, or damaged hair and would be labeled in such a way as to avoid confusion over what strength it is.

202. a. Thio relaxers are milder and may thus be used on hair that is damaged, finer, or less curly.

203. b. Take frequent test curls to ensure that the curls are forming properly but the hair is not being damaged.

204. c. A protective base is always used with a sodium hydroxide relaxer.

Hair Design

Haircutting

205. a. Section 1 begins at the front hairline and extends to the top of the head.

206. b. The thumb is inserted into the ring of the movable blade.

207. c. Slithering and effiliating both refer to thinning the hair.

208. d. After sectioning, decide on the length of the nape guideline hair, and cut.

209. a. Stand in front of the client in order to cut bangs straight.

210. c. As you cut each section, use the previously cut section as a guide.

211. b. Beveling is the technique used for creating fullness in a haircut by cutting the ends of the hair at a slight taper. It is most often used with blunt cuts.

212. d. A blunt cut has no layers and therefore employs no elevation.

213. d. The length of the hair cut is determined by the desired finished style.

214. b. The crown is the area between the apex and the back of the parietal ridge. It is important to identify any hair growth patterns in this area that may affect your finished cut.

215. c. A layered haircut is a graduated effect achieved by cutting the hair with elevation or overdirection. Layers create movement and volume in the hair by releasing weight.

216. c. The most important thing to remember when cutting curly hair is that curly hair behaves differently than straight hair after it is cut, for example it shrinks much more after it dries than straight hair.

217. c. Clippers are used to trim the client's neck hair.

Hair Styling

218. c. The correct procedure for forming the first ridge is to position the comb under your index finger and pull forward.

219. d. The first ridge begins at the hairline, and the second begins at the crown of the head.

220. a. The finished curl is not affected by the shape of the base. The other statements about pin curls are all correct.

221. a. Finer hair requires a larger number of pin curls.

222. c. Brushing is the next step after removing rollers and pins.

223. b. Back combing adds volume to a hairstyle.

224. d. For close-set eyes, create fullness at the top; the style should be fairly high with a side movement.

225. b. Long, full waves of hair will minimize a long, thin neck.

226. c. Balance a protruding chin by creating a hairstyle with fullness over the forehead.

227. b. Smooth rotating motions are essential to correct use of the thermal iron.

228. b. A full-base curl should be placed firmly in the center of its base.

229. a. Do not use a metal or celluloid comb; a metal comb can burn the client, and a celluloid comb can catch on fire.

230. a. The larger diameter the brush, the looser the curls.

231. a. An air waver is most successful if you locate and follow the hair's natural waves.

232. b. A blown-dry style will not hold if both the hair and scalp are not completely dry at the end of styling.

Thermal Hair Straightening

233. a. The size of the subsections is determined by the hair's texture, not by how curly it is.

234. c. Tinted or lightened hair is more likely to discolor when pressed.

235. a. With very short hair, take particular care to avoid burning the client's skin.

236. d. A hard press is a technique that removes 100% of the curl by applying the pressing comb twice on each side of the hair.

237. b. In the event of an accidental scalp burn, immediately apply 1% gentian violet jelly.

Braiding and Hair Extensions

238. a. It is best to braid hair when it is dry because if the hair is braided wet, it shrinks and recoils as it dries and may create excess pulling and tension.

239. c. A visible braid is a three-strand braid that employs the underhand technique, in which strands of hair are woven under the center strand.

240. b. Cornrows or canerows are narrow rows of visible braids that lie close to the scalp, worn by men, women, and children, and can be braided on hair of various lengths and textures. These flat contoured styles can last several weeks when applied without extensions, and up to two months when applied with extensions.

241. a. Hair locking, also called dreadlocks, is natural textured hair that is intertwined and meshed together to form a single or separate network of hair.

242. c. During the growing stage the bulb can be felt at the end of each lock and the hair grows longer.

243. c. To remove bonded wefts you must first dissolve the adhesive bond with oil or bond remover and then you can gently pull the weft from the hair.

244. d. Fusion is a good choice for clients with fine, limp hair because bonding and tracking create bulk at the base which is too bulky and obvious with fine hair.

245. **b.** The angle that the track is attached to the supporting braid is what will determine how the hair will fall.

Wigs and Hair Enhancements

246. **b.** The manufacturer needs information not only about the measurements and hair color, type, and length, but also about the hair parting and pattern.

247. **c.** The correct procedure for stretching a wig that is too small is to wet it, pin it to a larger block, and let it dry naturally.

248. **b.** It is often advisable to cut a wig while the client is wearing it.

249. **a.** Cut synthetic wigs while dry, and do not use a razor.

250. **b.** Use a wide-tooth comb to avoid damaging the hair of the wig.

5 ▶ Cosmetology Practice Exam 2

CHAPTER SUMMARY

This is the second of four practice exams based on the core content of your cosmetology coursework. Having taken one exam and having reviewed the Cosmetology Refresher Course, you should feel more confident about your ability to pick the correct answers. As you take this test, remember that knowing what to expect helps you feel better prepared.

L IKE THE FIRST 100-question exam in this book, this test is similar to the official cosmetology licensing exam that you will take. This time around, you know more about how the exam is put together because you have seen many sample multiple-choice questions and are perhaps beginning to notice patterns in the order of questions. For example, you see that questions in each content area are grouped together. This pattern will help you develop your own test-taking strategy.

If you're following the LearningExpress Test Preparation System, you have done some studying between the first exam and this one and have also practiced your test-taking skills in Chapter 4. This second exam will give you a chance to see how much you have improved.

As before, the answer sheet follows this page, and the test is followed by the answer key. Pay attention to the explanations in the answer key, especially for the questions you missed.

Practice Exam 2

1.	a	b	c	d	36.	a	b	c	d	71.	a	b	c	d
2.	a	b	c	d	37.	a	b	c	d	72.	a	b	c	d
3.	a	b	c	d	38.	a	b	c	d	73.	a	b	c	d
4.	a	b	c	d	39.	a	b	c	d	74.	a	b	c	d
5.	a	b	c	d	40.	a	b	c	d	75.	a	b	c	d
6.	a	b	c	d	41.	a	b	c	d	76.	a	b	c	d
7.	a	b	c	d	42.	a	b	c	d	77.	a	b	c	d
8.	a	b	c	d	43.	a	b	c	d	78.	a	b	c	d
9.	a	b	c	d	44.	a	b	c	d	79.	a	b	c	d
10.	a	b	c	d	45.	a	b	c	d	80.	a	b	c	d
11.	a	b	c	d	46.	a	b	c	d	81.	a	b	c	d
12.	a	b	c	d	47.	a	b	c	d	82.	a	b	c	d
13.	a	b	c	d	48.	a	b	c	d	83.	a	b	c	d
14.	a	b	c	d	49.	a	b	c	d	84.	a	b	c	d
15.	a	b	c	d	50.	a	b	c	d	85.	a	b	c	d
16.	a	b	c	d	51.	a	b	c	d	86.	a	b	c	d
17.	a	b	c	d	52.	a	b	c	d	87.	a	b	c	d
18.	a	b	c	d	53.	a	b	c	d	88.	a	b	c	d
19.	a	b	c	d	54.	a	b	c	d	89.	a	b	c	d
20.	a	b	c	d	55.	a	b	c	d	90.	a	b	c	d
21.	a	b	c	d	56.	a	b	c	d	91.	a	b	c	d
22.	a	b	c	d	57.	a	b	c	d	92.	a	b	c	d
23.	a	b	c	d	58.	a	b	c	d	93.	a	b	c	d
24.	a	b	c	d	59.	a	b	c	d	94.	a	b	c	d
25.	a	b	c	d	60.	a	b	c	d	95.	a	b	c	d
26.	a	b	c	d	61.	a	b	c	d	96.	a	b	c	d
27.	a	b	c	d	62.	a	b	c	d	97.	a	b	c	d
28.	a	b	c	d	63.	a	b	c	d	98.	a	b	c	d
29.	a	b	c	d	64.	a	b	c	d	99.	a	b	c	d
30.	a	b	c	d	65.	a	b	c	d	100.	a	b	c	d
31.	a	b	c	d	66.	a	b	c	d					
32.	a	b	c	d	67.	a	b	c	d					
33.	a	b	c	d	68.	a	b	c	d					
34.	a	b	c	d	69.	a	b	c	d					
35.	a	b	c	d	70.	a	b	c	d					

▶ Practice Exam 2

1. The daily maintenance of personal cleanliness and healthfulness is known as
   a. personal hygiene.
   b. preventive healthcare.
   c. cosmetology.
   d. relaxation.

2. The most important thing to consider when selecting shoes to wear at work is
   a. comfort.
   b. color.
   c. style.
   d. quality of leather.

3. When working with a client, you should AVOID
   a. sarcastic remarks.
   b. gentle encouragement.
   c. polite chitchat.
   d. tolerance and understanding.

4. If you must cough or sneeze while you are with a client, you should
   a. cover your nose and mouth.
   b. say "excuse me" first.
   c. leave the room.
   d. wear a face mask.

5. Cosmetologists need to understand bacteriology in order to
   a. prevent the spread of disease.
   b. discuss biology with clients.
   c. avoid contracting food-borne illnesses.
   d. avoid spreading AIDS in the salon.

6. Which microorganisms are unable to move on their own and are spread through the air?
   a. treponema
   b. microspira
   c. mycobacterium tuberculosis
   d. streptococci

7. In a salon, contagious disease may be spread through direct contact between people or through use of
   a. very hot or very cold water.
   b. unsanitary tools and supplies.
   c. infection control procedures.
   d. nonpathogenic bacteria.

8. Which statement about contamination is correct?
   a. All everyday objects are contaminated with microorganisms.
   b. Contamination can be avoided by means of frequent handwashing.
   c. Contamination in the salon is illegal and cause for losing one's license.
   d. The skin and hair can be sterilized to reduce contamination.

9. The Material Safety Data Sheet for a disinfectant will tell you
   a. why it is necessary to use disinfectants.
   b. how to market the product to your clients.
   c. whether it is safe to use the product on your skin.
   d. the content, associated hazards, and storage requirements.

10. In a salon, commercial disinfectants, such as Lysol or Pine-Sol, are used to
    a. wash hands.
    b. launder gowns.
    c. sterilize instruments and tools
    d. clean floors and countertops.

11. The purpose of universal sanitation is to
    a. create a safe environment.
    b. prevent the spread of AIDS.
    c. prevent lawsuits.
    d. create the impression that the salon is clean.

12. The hair root is located
    a. above the skin's surface.
    b. below the skin's surface.
    c. on the outside of the hair shaft.
    d. on the inside of the hair shaft.

13. Seen in cross section, wavy hair appears to be
    a. round.
    b. oval.
    c. almost flat.
    d. completely flat.

14. Which statement about hair is correct?
    a. Cutting the hair very short increases the rate of growth.
    b. Applying oils or creams can increase the rate of hair growth.
    c. Hair growth is most rapid in a person's young adult years.
    d. A person's hair continues to grow after his or her death.

15. The purpose of a general scalp treatment is to
    a. cure infectious skin conditions.
    b. keep the scalp and hair healthy.
    c. eliminate dandruff and itchy scalp.
    d. prepare the client for electrolysis.

16. Your client has round, red patches on her scalp and brittle hair that is broken off at the base in many places. You should refer this client to a physician for treatment of
    a. favus.
    b. ringworm.
    c. scabies.
    d. head lice.

17. The part of the nail structure that contains actively growing tissue is the
    a. nail plate.
    b. matrix.
    c. nail root.
    d. free edge.

18. You should **NOT** manicure a nail that shows signs of
    a. atrophy.
    b. pterygium.
    c. white spots.
    d. onychomycosis.

19. Corrugations and furrows in the nail can be caused by pregnancy, illness, or
    a. injury.
    b. heart disease.
    c. infection.
    d. nerves.

20. The human skin is thinnest over the
    a. soles of the feet.
    b. palms of the hands.
    c. eyelids.
    d. ears.

21. A mosquito bite is an example of which type of skin lesion?
   a. cyst
   b. macule
   c. papule
   d. weal

22. Your client has developed several persistent, moist lesions on her face and arms. You should suggest that the client
   a. try lotions appropriate for oily skin.
   b. try a glycolic peel.
   c. see a doctor for diagnosis and treatment.
   d. consult a cosmetology textbook.

23. Parasites cause disease when they invade plant or animal tissue and belong to this group of bacteria:
   a. nonpathogenic
   b. muscle reducing
   c. pathogenic
   d. virus

24. What kind of muscle are the muscles in the arms and legs?
   a. involuntary muscle
   b. voluntary muscle
   c. smooth muscle
   d. cardiac muscle

25. The muscles located in the hand are the
   a. trapezius and latissimus dorsi muscles.
   b. abductors, adductors, and opponent muscles.
   c. pectoralis major and minor and serratus anterior muscles.
   d. biceps, triceps, and deltoid muscles.

26. The large blood vessel that supplies blood to the head, face, and neck is the
   a. carotid artery.
   b. jugular vein.
   c. angular artery.
   d. angular vein.

27. Which of the following is **NOT** a safe way to use electricity?
   a. plugging only one appliance into each outlet
   b. replacing blown-out fuses with fresh ones
   c. checking electric cords regularly for fraying
   d. handling electric equipment with wet hands

28. When using ultraviolet rays, the cosmetologist and the client should always wear
   a. sunscreen.
   b. safety glasses.
   c. rubber gloves.
   d. long sleeves.

29. A whitish discoloration of the nails, caused by injury to the base of the nail is called
   a. leukonychia.
   b. melanonychia.
   c. onychatrophia.
   d. pterygium.

30. Humectants, which temporarily attract and hold moisture, are an important ingredient in
   a. protein conditioners.
   b. instant conditioners.
   c. shampoos.
   d. neutralizers.

31. The chemical reaction that occurs when hair is bleached lighter is the
   a. formation of a melanin solution.
   b. dilution of a melanin solution.
   c. diaphoresis of melanin.
   d. oxidation of melanin.

32. Moisturizing creams work by
   a. creating a barrier that lets the skin's natural fluids accumulate.
   b. forcing moisture to enter the skin through a chemical reaction.
   c. bonding with the skin's natural oil and moisture.
   d. stimulating the skin to produce additional moisture.

33. Which of the following is a way for a beauty professional to become his or her own boss?
   a. deciding to rent a booth
   b. working as a massage therapist in an existing salon
   c. becoming the salon manager of an elite day spa
   d. becoming a cosmetology instructor

34. An agreement to buy an established salon should include all of the following EXCEPT a
   a. business plan for the next five years.
   b. written purchase agreement.
   c. statement of whether the new owner may use the salon's name.
   d. statement that the former owner will not open a competing salon.

35. To ensure that clients look forward to their next visit, your salon operations need to be
   a. inexpensive.
   b. well-organized.
   c. on the cutting edge of style.
   d. rigid.

36. The two most important principles behind a successful sale are to know your merchandise and to
   a. adapt your sales pitch to the client's needs.
   b. tell the client anything he or she wants to hear.
   c. always assume that the client knows nothing about the product.
   d. sell additional products.

37. You have just draped a client for hair cutting. The reason that you remove the outer towel and replace it with a neck strip is to
   a. keep the client from becoming overheated.
   b. make the client look more attractive.
   c. protect the client's face and neck.
   d. allow the hair to fall to the floor.

38. Before applying chemicals to the hair, you should apply a cream around the client's hairline in order to
   a. avoid a lawsuit.
   b. test for allergic reaction.
   c. sell additional products.
   d. avoid skin irritation.

39. Soft water is preferable to hard water for shampooing because it
   a. holds its temperature better.
   b. works up a better lather.
   c. feels softer on the client's skin.
   d. does not contain minerals.

40. The purpose of hair brushing is to stimulate the scalp and to
   a. provide a substitute for a scalp massage.
   b. provide a substitute for a shampoo.
   c. loosen natural curls and change the hair's texture.
   d. remove dust, dirt, and hairspray buildup.

41. The professional cosmetologist's responsibility regarding shampoo products is to
a. sell a large number of different products.
b. select the right one for each client.
c. have a complete understanding of shampoo chemistry.
d. encourage the client to make her own choices.

42. How do you remove light-cured gel nails?
a. soak them in acetone
b. buff them layer by layer
c. pour adhesive over them
d. apply acetone and put them under a UV light source

43. Nail hardeners are applied just before the
a. cuticles are cut.
b. base coat is applied.
c. nail dryer is applied.
d. polish is applied.

44. When removing old nail polish, you should AVOID
a. chipping the polish.
b. getting the nails wet.
c. smearing polish onto the cuticles.
d. using too much nail polish remover.

45. The purpose of a hand massage is to
a. earn money for the salon
b. make the client's hands relaxed and flexible
c. make nail polish adhere better
d. impress the client with your knowledge and skill

46. A discoloration in the natural nail after sculptured nails are applied usually indicates that the
a. nail has developed a fungus infection.
b. sculptured nail is correctly bonded to the natural nail.
c. client needs a darker shade of polish.
d. natural nail has died.

47. The two basins used for soaking a client's feet before a pedicure contain
a. warm water in one and cold water in the other.
b. cold water in both.
c. antiseptic solution in one and warm water in the other.
d. antiseptic solution in one and disinfectant in the other.

48. The correct direction in which to massage a muscle is from the
a. point of insertion to the point of origin.
b. middle to the point of insertion.
c. middle to the point of origin.
d. point of origin to the point of insertion.

49. You should avoid vigorous massage of joints if your client
a. is elderly.
b. is overweight.
c. has diabetes.
d. has arthritis.

50. The cosmetologist's knowledge of skin diseases should consist of
a. when to advise a client to seek medical treatment.
b. what lotions to apply for each condition.
c. what corrective measures to take.
d. when to use electrical or ultraviolet therapy.

51. The primary purpose of steaming the face is to
a. open the pores.
b. tighten the muscles.
c. clean the skin.
d. eliminate wrinkles.

52. For a client with dry skin, you should avoid the use of
a. infrared rays.
b. galvanic current.
c. lotions containing alcohol.
d. facial masks or packs.

53. Gauze, or cheesecloth, is used to hold mask ingredients that
a. would be messy if applied directly to the skin.
b. are too acidic to come in direct contact with the skin.
c. are very hot or cold.
d. would be very expensive if used on their own.

54. Before applying facial makeup for a client, you should be sure that your hands are clean and that
a. the client has signed a release form.
b. all applicators are sanitized or new.
c. you agree with the client's color choices.
d. the client's hair care procedures are completed.

55. Before applying cheek color, you should ask the client to
a. frown.
b. smile.
c. laugh.
d. suck in her cheeks.

56. Corrective makeup for a bulging forehead consists of applying
a. darker foundation over the prominent area.
b. lighter foundation within the prominent area.
c. lighter foundation below the prominent area.
d. darker foundation all around the prominent area.

57. If eyeliner is to be used along with artificial eyelashes, the cosmetologist usually
a. draws on the eyeliner after the lashes are in place.
b. draws the eyeliner first, then retouches after applying the lashes.
c. draws on the eyeliner only after applying the artificial eyelashes.
d. applies eyeliner to the bottom lid only.

58. Another name for the commonly used short-wave method of permanent hair removal is
a. electrolysis.
b. thermolysis.
c. epilosis.
d. the blend method.

59. What type of hair removal is a laser beam that is pulsed on the skin, impairing the hair follicles?
a. waxing
b. lasering
c. sugaring
d. epilating

60. The main active ingredient in acid-balanced waving lotions is
a. ammonium thioglycolate.
b. glycerol monothioglycolate.
c. hydrogen peroxide.
d. hydrogen disulfide.

61. On which type of hair should you use an acid-balanced perm?
   a. coarse, resistant hair
   b. highlighted or tinted hair
   c. normal hair
   d. fine, resistant hair

62. A curl that rests on base after winding will produce the greatest degree of
   a. fullness.
   b. tightness.
   c. smoothness.
   d. glossiness.

63. If a client wants both a perm and hair coloring, you should
   a. tint the hair first, then perm it later the same day.
   b. perm the hair first, then tint it one week later.
   c. apply both chemicals at the same time.
   d. perform either procedure first, but wait at least a day before doing the second.

64. At what temperature do alkaline waves process?
   a. heated temperature
   b. room temperature
   c. freezing temperature
   d. below zero temperature

65. A patch test to determine whether a client is allergic to an aniline derivative tint should be carried out
   a. immediately before the hair coloring is done.
   b. one hour before the hair coloring is done.
   c. 24–28 hours before the hair coloring is done.
   d. immediately after the hair coloring is done.

66. Cool-toned colors are those in which
   a. blue predominates.
   b. red predominates.
   c. yellow predominates.
   d. no black is present.

67. Approximately how long do deposit-only hair coloring products last?
   a. 1–2 weeks
   b. 2–4 weeks
   c. 4–6 weeks
   d. 6–8 weeks

68. The correct procedure for applying lightener to the hair shaft is to begin
   a. at the root and apply liberally down to the ends.
   b. one-half inch from the scalp and work down to the ends.
   c. in the middle and stop one-half inch from the ends and one-half inch from the scalp.
   d. at the ends and work to within one inch of the scalp.

69. The oxidizing agent that, when mixed with an oxidative haircolor, supplies the necessary oxygen gas to develop color molecules and create a change in hair color is called
   a. formulator.
   b. developer.
   c. constructor.
   d. regulator.

70. You are covering the gray hair in your client's salt-and-pepper hair. You should select a shade that is
   a. darker than the natural dark hair.
   b. the same as the natural shade.
   c. lighter than the natural shade.
   d. a blend of the natural shade and the gray tone.

71. The chemical process involving the diffusion of the natural color pigment or artificial color from the hair is called hair
  a. coloring.
  b. streaking.
  c. glazing.
  d. lightening.

72. The Level System is a way of analyzing the
  a. tone of a hair color.
  b. texture of the hair.
  c. absence or presence of pigment in the hair.
  d. lightness or darkness of a color.

73. The primary colors are
  a. green, purple, and orange.
  b. red, blue, and green.
  c. red, brown, and yellow.
  d. blue, red, and yellow.

74. Semipermanent hair colors are a good choice for a client who
  a. wishes to go only one shade lighter.
  b. has selected a difficult-to-achieve shade.
  c. wants the color to last only until the next shampoo.
  d. is just beginning to turn gray.

75. A double-process application of hair color involves the use of a lightener plus
  a. a toner or tint.
  b. a semipermanent hair color.
  c. a mousse.
  d. hydrogen peroxide.

76. When draping a client for a haircolor service be sure **NOT** to
  a. slide a towel down from the back of the client's head and place lengthwise across the client's shoulders.
  b. cross the ends of the towel beneath the chin and place the cape over the towel.
  c. leave the cape open in the back for comfort.
  d. fold the towel over the top of the cape and secure in front.

77. The purpose of the petroleum cream in "base" formula hair relaxers is to
  a. increase the speed of the reaction.
  b. decrease the heat of the reaction.
  c. protect the client's skin and scalp.
  d. protect the cosmetologist's hands.

78. When applying relaxer to the client's hair, you would
  a. massage it into the entire head with your palms and fingers.
  b. apply it to the scalp first and stretch each strand out tight.
  c. spread it out evenly over the top and bottom of each small strand.
  d. brush it vigorously through each section of hair with a wire brush.

79. You should **NOT** give a soft-curl perm to a client whose hair has been
  a. relaxed with sodium hydroxide.
  b. bleached with peroxide.
  c. tinted.
  d. given a conditioning treatment.

80. A good hairstyle will accentuate the client's good features while it
  a. costs a great deal of money.
  b. changes the texture of the hair.
  c. minimizes the negative ones.
  d. takes a very short time.

81. The purpose of thinning a client's hair is to
  a. remove excess bulk.
  b. make hair less curly.
  c. make hair appear fuller.
  d. improve the texture of hair.

82. Which of these are two basic lines used in haircutting?
  a. straight and round
  b. straight and curve
  c. straight and diagonal
  d. diagonal and curved

83. What type of lines are used to create one-length and low-elevation haircuts because they build weight?
  a. diagonal
  b. horizontal
  c. curved
  d. vertical

84. Before cutting section 2 at the crown of the head, you would divide it
  a. into three vertical strips.
  b. into pie-shaped wedges.
  c. horizontally.
  d. into four quarters.

85. Which of the following is **NOT** a type of stitch used to sew the extension to the track?
  a. lock stitch
  b. double-lock stitch
  c. bonding stitch
  d. overcast stitch

86. Finger waves will **NOT** remain in place if the hair is combed out
  a. after the waving lotion is applied.
  b. after the hair net is put on.
  c. before the hair is completely dry.
  d. before the left side is waved.

87. Which part of the pin curl gives the curl its direction and mobility?
  a. base
  b. stem
  c. circle
  d. clip

88. You can create a longer-lasting curl by
  a. stretching the hair strand and applying tension.
  b. using very small amounts of hair in each strand.
  c. making the pin curl very wide.
  d. rotating the pin curl counterclockwise.

89. Which of these is **NOT** a basic method of locking?
  a. comb technique
  b. the palm roll
  c. color locking
  d. braids or extensions

90. In designing a hairstyle for a client with a round face, you should aim to
  a. add the illusion of height to the face.
  b. create the illusion of length to the hair.
  c. create the illusion of width in the forehead.
  d. reduce the width across the cheekbones.

91. A curved rectangular part, with bangs, is often used for a client with a
a. receding hairline
b. very strong natural part.
c. prominent chin.
d. round or square face.

92. What type of hair can tolerate the most heat when thermal waving?
a. chemically treated hair
b. tinted hair
c. gray hair
d. fine hair

93. Which type of thermal curl provides a strong curl with full, but not maximum, volume?
a. volume-base curl
b. full-base curl
c. half-base curl
d. off-base curl

94. To test the temperature of curling irons, you should use
a. tissue paper
b. a concealed lock of the client's hair
c. your own hair
d. your fingers

95. Styling lotions or gels are used in blow drying to
a. hold the hair firmly in place.
b. make the hair dry faster.
c. avoid damage and split ends.
d. make the hair manageable.

96. A thermal hair straightening treatment lasts until the
a. client's next shampoo.
b. hair grows out.
c. hair is combed or brushed.
d. client's next haircut.

97. Before you place the pressing comb on the hair, you should test its temperature on
a. cloth or paper.
b. the client's face.
c. your hand.
d. a rubber comb.

98. The surest way to distinguish human hair from synthetic hair is to test how it
a. feels.
b. smells.
c. looks.
d. burns.

99. Because hand-made wigs have a delicate structure and are easily damaged, you should clean them
a. on a block.
b. on the client's head.
c. at the dry cleaners.
d. as seldom as possible.

100. Which statement about coloring a wig is correct?
a. Color rinses can either lighten or darken the hair.
b. Wigs and hairpieces can be bleached just like real hair.
c. Permanent tints can be used successfully on human hair wigs and hairpieces.
d. Semipermanent tints can be applied successful to machine-made wigs.

► Answers

1. **a.** Personal hygiene includes all the activities you undertake daily to maintain your health and cleanliness.

2. **a.** Although you should wear stylish shoes at work, cosmetologists, who spend most of the day on their feet, should select shoes for comfort.

3. **a.** Avoid sarcastic or disapproving remarks or gestures when dealing with clients.

4. **a.** Cover your nose and mouth if you cough or sneeze.

5. **a.** It is important for you to understand bacteriology so that you can help prevent the spread of diseases. (AIDS is not caused by bacteria.)

6. **d.** Cocci, such as staphylococci and streptococci, are unable to move on their own and are usually spread through the air, through dust, or by touching infected material.

7. **b.** In a salon, disease can be spread by use of unsanitary tools and supplies.

8. **a.** Everything you touch is contaminated with microorganisms.

9. **d.** The Material Safety Data Sheet tells you all the pertinent information including how to safely use and store the disinfectant.

10. **d.** Commercial cleaners may be used for ordinary cleaning, such as washing floors and countertops, but should not be used on tools.

11. **a.** Universal sanitation creates a safe environment for both clients and salon workers.

12. **b.** The hair root is the part located below the skin's surface.

13. **b.** In cross section, wavy hair is oval.

14. **c.** Hair growth is most rapid between the ages of 20 and 30.

15. **b.** General scalp treatments maintain healthy scalp and hair.

16. **b.** The client has symptoms of ringworm.

17. **b.** The matrix is the part of the nail structure that contains actively growing tissue.

18. **d.** Onychomycosis refers to a fungus infection of the nail.

19. **a.** Systemic illness and injury to the nailbed are the most common causes.

20. **c.** The skin is thinnest and most delicate over the eyelids.

21. **d.** A mosquito bite is a weal—an itchy, swollen lesion.

22. **c.** Clients with skin diseases should be referred to a doctor.

23. **c.** Parasites cause disease when they invade plant or animal tissue and belong to the pathogenic category.

24. **b.** The muscles in the arms, legs, and face are voluntary, or striated, muscle.

25. **b.** This choice lists the major muscle groups of the hand.

26. **a.** The carotid artery and its many branches supply blood to the neck, face, and head, including the brain.

27. **d.** Handling electrical equipment with wet hands is an unsafe practice, since water is a conductor.

28. **b.** To avoid damage to the eyes, always wear safety glasses or goggles for ultraviolet therapy.

29. **a.** Leukonychia is a whitish discoloration of the nails, caused by injury to the base of the nail.

30. **b.** Instant conditioners commonly contain humectants such as sorbitol and ethylene glycol.

31. **d.** The oxidation of melanin, caused by the action of hydrogen peroxide, causes the hair to bleach lighter.

32. **a.** Moisturizers create a barrier that holds the skin's natural oil and water in.

33. **a.** The two main options for becoming your own boss are opening a salon or renting a booth in an existing salon.

34. a. A purchase agreement would not include a business plan, which is a separate document.

35. b. A well-organized salon promotes a client's confidence and comfort.

36. a. The most successful salesperson always adapts her sales pitch to the individual client's needs and personality.

37. d. If you kept the outer towel on, it would catch the cut hair and prevent it from falling to the floor.

38. d. The purpose of applying a protective cream around the hairline is to avoid skin irritation.

39. b. Soft water is preferable for shampooing because it works up a better lather.

40. d. Brushing removes dirt and debris from the hair.

41. b. Your responsibility is to select the right shampoo for each client.

42. b. Light cured gel nails can only be removed by buffing them layer-by-layer and will not soak off in acetone.

43. b. Nail hardener is applied just before the base coat.

44. c. Avoid smearing polish onto the cuticles or surrounding tissues.

45. b. The hand massage will make the client's hands relaxed, flexible, and supple.

46. a. Discoloration indicates that the natural nail has developed a fungus infection.

47. c. Soak the client's feet first in antiseptic solution and then in plain warm water.

48. a. Massage a muscle from the point of insertion to the point of origin.

49. d. Avoid vigorous massage of joints if your client has arthritis, since you are likely to cause the client pain.

50. a. Cosmetologists do not treat skin diseases, but they must recognize when a client should seek treatment from a doctor.

51. a. The primary purpose of facial steaming is to open the pores for deep cleansing; steaming also improves blood circulation.

52. c. Lotions containing alcohol can cause additional dryness.

53. a. Gauze is used to hold ingredients, such as crushed fruits, that would be messy if applied directly.

54. b. Use only applicators that have been sanitized or that are new and disposable.

55. b. Ask the client to smile; this will make her cheeks prominent and show where the color should be placed.

56. a. To minimize the bulging forehead, cover it with a darker shade of foundation than that used on the rest of the face.

57. b. Drawing the eyeliner before applying the lashes, and then retouching, is the correct procedure.

58. b. Thermolysis, or the short-wave method, is the most commonly used today.

59. b. Laser hair removal is a removal treatment in which a laser beam is pulsed on the skin, impairing the hair follicles.

60. b. The main active ingredient is glycerol monothioglycolate.

61. b. Tinted or highlighted hair should generally receive an acid-balanced perm.

62. a. Curls that are held on base start close to the head and thus produce the greatest degree of height and fullness.

63. b. Perm the hair first, and then tint it no sooner than one week later.

64. b. Alkaline waves process at room temperature.

65. c. A patch test must be done 24–28 hours before the hair coloring is scheduled.

66. a. Cool-toned colors are those in which blue predominates.

67. c. Deposit-only hair coloring products last approximately 4 to 6 weeks.

68. b. The correct procedure is one-half inch from the scalp and work down to the ends.

69. b. A developer is an oxidizing agent that, when mixed with an oxidative haircolor, supplies the necessary oxygen gas to develop color molecules and create a change in hair color.

70. c. Because color on color makes a darker color, select a shade that is lighter than the natural hair color.

71. d. Hair lightening is a chemical process involving the diffusion of the natural color pigment or artificial color from the hair, making it appear lighter.

72. d. The Level System is a way of analyzing the darkness or lightness of a color, independent of tone.

73. d. All other colors can be achieved by mixing these three colors.

74. d. Semipermanent colors are a good choice for a client who is just beginning to go gray, since they can even out the hair tones without changing the underlying color.

75. a. A double-process application involves the use of a lightener plus a toner or a tint.

76. c. The cape must be fastened securely in the back to ensure that it doesn't slip or move during the service.

77. c. The petroleum cream base protects the client's skin and scalp, and in the case of a retouch, previously treated hair as well.

78. c. Spread the relaxer over the top and bottom of each strand with the back of a comb or with your hands.

79. a. Do not give a soft-curl perm, which uses thio, to a client whose hair has been treated with sodium hydroxide.

80. c. A good hairstyle will accentuate the good features and minimize the negative ones.

81. a. Thinning hair removes excess bulk.

82. b. Straight lines are used to cut over flat surfaces on the head and curved lines are used to cut over rounded surfaces of the head shape.

83. b. Horizontal lines are used to create one-length and low-elevation haircuts because they build weight with no graduation.

84. b. Section 2 is divided into pie-shaped wedges.

85. c. Bonding involves attaching hair wefts or single strands with an adhesive or a glue gun.

86. c. Do not comb out the waves until the hair is completely dry.

87. b. The stem of the curl gives it its mobility, action, and direction.

88. a. Stretching and applying tension results in longer-lasting curls.

89. c. The three basic methods of locking are the comb technique, which involves placing the comb at the base of the scalp and, with a rotating motion, spiraling the hair into a curl, the palm roll, which involves applying gel to dampened subsections, placing the portion of hair between the palms of both hands, and rolling in a clockwise or counter-clockwise direction; and braids or extensions, which involves sectioning the hair for the desired size lock and single braiding the hair to the end.

90. a. For a client with a round face, attempt to create an illusion of greater height to the face.

91. a. A curved rectangular part that sets off bangs is used for a receding hairline or very high forehead.

92. c. Hair that is gray or very coarse can tolerate the most heat.

93. b. A full-base curl is used to create a strong curl with full volume.

94. a. Use tissue paper to test the temperature of the curling irons.

95. d. Styling lotions and gels make the hair more manageable for blow drying.

96. a. Thermal hair pressing (hair straightening) lasts only until the next shampoo.

97. a. Make sure that the pressing comb is not too hot by holding it against a piece of white cloth or paper and checking for burning.

98. d. Synthetic hair burns quickly and gives off little or no odor, in contrast to human hair, which burns slowly and gives off a very distinct odor.

99. a. Keep a hand-made wig on a block at all times while you clean it.

100. d. The other statements are incorrect.

Cosmetology Practice Exam 3

CHAPTER SUMMARY

This is the third of four practice exams in this book that are based on the core content of your cosmetology coursework. Use this test to identify which types of questions are still giving you problems.

YOU ARE NOW beginning to be very familiar with the format of cosmetology exams. Your practice test-taking experience will help you most, however, if you have created a study situation as close as possible to the real testing experience.

For this third exam, simulate the official test. Find a quiet place where you will not be disturbed. Have two sharpened pencils with good erasers on hand. Complete the test in one sitting, setting a timer or a stopwatch for two hours. You should have plenty of time to answer all of the questions when you take the real exam, but you should practice working quickly, without rushing.

As before, the answer sheet is on the next page. Following the exam is the answer key, with all of the answers explained. These explanations will help you see where you need to concentrate further study. When you've finished the exam and scored it, turn back to Chapter 1 to see which questions correspond with which areas of your cosmetology coursework—then you will know which parts of your textbook to focus on before you take the fourth and final practice exam in this book.

Practice Exam 3

1.	(a)	(b)	(c)	(d)	36.	(a)	(b)	(c)	(d)	71.	(a)	(b)	(c)	(d)
2.	(a)	(b)	(c)	(d)	37.	(a)	(b)	(c)	(d)	72.	(a)	(b)	(c)	(d)
3.	(a)	(b)	(c)	(d)	38.	(a)	(b)	(c)	(d)	73.	(a)	(b)	(c)	(d)
4.	(a)	(b)	(c)	(d)	39.	(a)	(b)	(c)	(d)	74.	(a)	(b)	(c)	(d)
5.	(a)	(b)	(c)	(d)	40.	(a)	(b)	(c)	(d)	75.	(a)	(b)	(c)	(d)
6.	(a)	(b)	(c)	(d)	41.	(a)	(b)	(c)	(d)	76.	(a)	(b)	(c)	(d)
7.	(a)	(b)	(c)	(d)	42.	(a)	(b)	(c)	(d)	77.	(a)	(b)	(c)	(d)
8.	(a)	(b)	(c)	(d)	43.	(a)	(b)	(c)	(d)	78.	(a)	(b)	(c)	(d)
9.	(a)	(b)	(c)	(d)	44.	(a)	(b)	(c)	(d)	79.	(a)	(b)	(c)	(d)
10.	(a)	(b)	(c)	(d)	45.	(a)	(b)	(c)	(d)	80.	(a)	(b)	(c)	(d)
11.	(a)	(b)	(c)	(d)	46.	(a)	(b)	(c)	(d)	81.	(a)	(b)	(c)	(d)
12.	(a)	(b)	(c)	(d)	47.	(a)	(b)	(c)	(d)	82.	(a)	(b)	(c)	(d)
13.	(a)	(b)	(c)	(d)	48.	(a)	(b)	(c)	(d)	83.	(a)	(b)	(c)	(d)
14.	(a)	(b)	(c)	(d)	49.	(a)	(b)	(c)	(d)	84.	(a)	(b)	(c)	(d)
15.	(a)	(b)	(c)	(d)	50.	(a)	(b)	(c)	(d)	85.	(a)	(b)	(c)	(d)
16.	(a)	(b)	(c)	(d)	51.	(a)	(b)	(c)	(d)	86.	(a)	(b)	(c)	(d)
17.	(a)	(b)	(c)	(d)	52.	(a)	(b)	(c)	(d)	87.	(a)	(b)	(c)	(d)
18.	(a)	(b)	(c)	(d)	53.	(a)	(b)	(c)	(d)	88.	(a)	(b)	(c)	(d)
19.	(a)	(b)	(c)	(d)	54.	(a)	(b)	(c)	(d)	89.	(a)	(b)	(c)	(d)
20.	(a)	(b)	(c)	(d)	55.	(a)	(b)	(c)	(d)	90.	(a)	(b)	(c)	(d)
21.	(a)	(b)	(c)	(d)	56.	(a)	(b)	(c)	(d)	91.	(a)	(b)	(c)	(d)
22.	(a)	(b)	(c)	(d)	57.	(a)	(b)	(c)	(d)	92.	(a)	(b)	(c)	(d)
23.	(a)	(b)	(c)	(d)	58.	(a)	(b)	(c)	(d)	93.	(a)	(b)	(c)	(d)
24.	(a)	(b)	(c)	(d)	59.	(a)	(b)	(c)	(d)	94.	(a)	(b)	(c)	(d)
25.	(a)	(b)	(c)	(d)	60.	(a)	(b)	(c)	(d)	95.	(a)	(b)	(c)	(d)
26.	(a)	(b)	(c)	(d)	61.	(a)	(b)	(c)	(d)	96.	(a)	(b)	(c)	(d)
27.	(a)	(b)	(c)	(d)	62.	(a)	(b)	(c)	(d)	97.	(a)	(b)	(c)	(d)
28.	(a)	(b)	(c)	(d)	63.	(a)	(b)	(c)	(d)	98.	(a)	(b)	(c)	(d)
29.	(a)	(b)	(c)	(d)	64.	(a)	(b)	(c)	(d)	99.	(a)	(b)	(c)	(d)
30.	(a)	(b)	(c)	(d)	65.	(a)	(b)	(c)	(d)	100.	(a)	(b)	(c)	(d)
31.	(a)	(b)	(c)	(d)	66.	(a)	(b)	(c)	(d)					
32.	(a)	(b)	(c)	(d)	67.	(a)	(b)	(c)	(d)					
33.	(a)	(b)	(c)	(d)	68.	(a)	(b)	(c)	(d)					
34.	(a)	(b)	(c)	(d)	69.	(a)	(b)	(c)	(d)					
35.	(a)	(b)	(c)	(d)	70.	(a)	(b)	(c)	(d)					

▶ Practice Exam 3

1. As a cosmetologist, it is important for you to wear stylish clothing that
   a. looks expensive.
   b. reflects the image of the salon.
   c. makes you look better than your coworkers.
   d. makes you seem younger than your coworkers.

2. Substances that can impair your health include
   a. soap.
   b. lotion.
   c. tobacco.
   d. fruit.

3. Part of effective communication skills for a cosmetologist includes
   a. telling the client what's best for him or her.
   b. avoiding needless talking while at work.
   c. understanding what the client wants.
   d. ignoring the client's wishes while seeming to listen politely.

4. Maintaining professional behavior with clients includes
   a. criticizing your coworkers' work and behavior.
   b. adapting your behavior to the client.
   c. forcefully attempting to sell extra beauty products.
   d. never speaking unless the client speaks first.

5. The bacteria that cause abscesses, boils, and pustules are
   a. streptococci.
   b. diplococci.
   c. treponema.
   d. staphylococci.

6. Which disease is caused by a virus?
   a. tuberculosis
   b. the common cold
   c. strep throat
   d. pediculosis

7. The best way to prevent the spread of infection in the salon is to
   a. sterilize all equipment and furniture between clients.
   b. practice good personal hygiene and sanitation.
   c. drink large amounts of water and eat a healthy diet.
   d. take a multi-vitamin.

8. Which of the following lives only by penetrating cells and becoming part of them?
   a. virus
   b. bacteria
   c. organisms
   d. amoebas

9. Hospital-level disinfectants are effective at killing
   a. viruses only.
   b. fungi only.
   c. bacteria and fungi.
   d. bacteria and viruses.

10. Which statement about the use of household bleach as a disinfectant is correct?
    a. Bleach is an effective disinfectant when mixed with alcohol.
    b. Bleach must be used full-strength to be an effective disinfectant.
    c. Bleach has been replaced by more modern disinfectants.
    d. Bleach may be used safely on all materials and fabrics.

11. Ultrasonic cleaners are used
   a. to disinfect materials on which disinfectants don't work.
   b. as an addition to the disinfection process.
   c. in place of disinfectants.
   d. on clients who are having pedicures.

12. The tubelike opening in the skin or scalp that surrounds the hair root is referred to as the
   a. epidermis.
   b. dermis.
   c. papilla.
   d. follicle.

13. The direction of hair growth is referred to as a
   a. cowlick.
   b. natural part.
   c. whorl.
   d. hair stream.

14. The ability of the hair shaft to absorb moisture is
   a. porosity.
   b. elasticity.
   c. viscosity.
   d. pigmentation.

15. Which condition is sometimes treated in the salon with ultraviolet treatments?
   a. alopecia senilis
   b. alopecia premature
   c. alopecia areata
   d. tinea capitis

16. The part of the hair that extends above the skin surface is called the
   a. hair shaft.
   b. hair root.
   c. follicle.
   d. sebaceous gland.

17. The extension of the cuticle over the half-moon at the base of the nail is referred to as the
   a. lunula.
   b. mantle.
   c. eponychium.
   d. perionychium.

18. White spots in the nail are usually caused by
   a. poor nutrition.
   b. poor circulation.
   c. minor injury.
   d. fungus infection.

19. It is particularly important to treat the cuticles gently and push them back only with an orangewood stick if the client
   a. is pregnant.
   b. has injured nails.
   c. has a fungus infection.
   d. bites his or her nails.

20. The point where the nail plate meets the tip before it is glued to the nail is called the
   a. position stop.
   b. lanula.
   c. position go.
   d. matrix.

21. Your client's hands are so dry and chapped that cracks have developed in the skin. These cracks are referred to as
   a. excoriations.
   b. fissures.
   c. scars.
   d. ulcers.

22. Which of the following conditions is contagious?
a. herpes simplex
b. eczema
c. miliaria rubra
d. psoriasis

23. The skin and scalp are both examples of
a. muscular tissue.
b. connective tissue.
c. nerve tissue.
d. epithelial tissue.

24. Muscle tissue may be stimulated by all of the following EXCEPT
a. application of heat.
b. application of cold.
c. massage.
d. electric current.

25. The chief sensory nerve of the face is the
a. fourth cranial nerve.
b. fifth cranial nerve.
c. sixth cranial nerve.
d. seventh cranial nerve.

26. The main blood supply to the arm and hand flows through the
a. infra-orbital and frontal arteries.
b. radial and ulnar arteries.
c. vena cava and aorta.
d. carotid artery.

27. Your hair dryer has tripped a circuit breaker. You reset the circuit breaker, but it immediately breaks the circuit once again. The safest thing to do is to
a. call an electrician to locate the problem.
b. connect the appliance to another circuit.
c. use a coin to complete the circuit.
d. attempt to rewire the appliance.

28. In electrolysis the electric current is applied with a very fine, needle-shaped electrode that is inserted into each
a. cell.
b. hair follicle.
c. hair strand.
d. capillary.

29. The pH of normal hair is approximately
a. 3.5
b. 5.0
c. 6.5
d. 8.0

30. Which type of conditioner enters the cortex of the hair and replaces the keratin lost during chemical services?
a. instant conditioner
b. moisturizing conditioner
c. protein conditioner
d. hot oil conditioner

31. Which statement about color fillers is correct?
a. Fillers are used before chemical services to increase the hair's porosity.
b. Fillers attach to the carbohydrate component of the hair.
c. Fillers occupy the spaces left in the hair shaft after the diffusion of melanin.
d. Fillers are made exclusively of human hair derivatives.

32. The two categories of facial treatments are
a. melodic and corrective.
b. preservative and harmonious.
c. corrective and preservative.
d. melodic and preservative.

33. A lease is an agreement between
a. a building owner and a tenant.
b. a lawyer and a client.
c. an employer and an employee.
d. a client and a cosmetologist.

34. The most important thing you can do to protect yourself against being sued for malpractice is to
a. keep accurate records of your working hours.
b. be proficient in all important knowledge and skills.
c. make sure you have adequate malpractice insurance.
d. make sure that your employee contract is signed by two witnesses.

35. The client's impression of your salon begins with his or her greeting by the
a. owner.
b. cosmetologist.
c. manicurist.
d. receptionist.

36. Your client tells you that she is in a hurry and that she wants a very practical hairstyle. She talks to you very little. The best way to please this client is to
a. keep up the conversation at all times.
b. design an elaborate hairstyle with the hope of changing her mind.
c. work as quickly and as efficiently as possible.
d. explain everything in detail and ask a lot of questions.

37. The reason that you fold a towel over the client's gown when draping a client for chemical services is to
a. protect the client's skin and clothing.
b. prevent the client from becoming chilly.
c. allow the client's clipped hair to fall to the floor.
d. make the client look more attractive.

38. Draping for dry hair services consists of
a. a neck strip only.
b. a neck strip and cape only.
c. a towel, neck strip, and cape.
d. two towels, neck strip, and cape.

39. When selecting a shampoo for a client, you should choose one that
a. suits the client's hair type.
b. uses only natural ingredients.
c. will eliminate dandruff.
d. smells great.

40. The correct procedure for adjusting water temperature before shampooing is to
a. turn on the hot water first and gradually add cold water.
b. turn on both hot and cold water simultaneously.
c. turn on the cold water first and then adjust the hot water.
d. use a thermometer to obtain the client's preferred temperature.

41. The visible line that separates colored hair from newly grown hair is called
a. hyperpigmentation.
b. hypopigmentation.
c. line of demarcation.
d. line of decolorization.

42. Habitual use of cream rinses can
   a. make the hair healthy and lustrous.
   b. serve in place of chemical treatments.
   c. correct the pH of the scalp.
   d. make hair heavy and oily.

43. When should you clean your manicuring table?
   a. when a new client arrives and sits down
   b. after every three clients
   c. right after each manicure
   d. at the end of your shift

44. Before shaping a client's nails, you should
   a. discuss what shape the client desires.
   b. tell the client the shape and colors you prefer.
   c. soften the client's cuticles.
   d. clean and bleach the free edges of the nails.

45. An oil manicure is beneficial for clients with brittle nails and
   a. dry cuticles.
   b. vitamin deficiencies.
   c. nail diseases.
   d. dry, patchy skin on the hands.

46. What can you do to prevent a fungus infection from growing underneath a sculptured nail?
   a. wear rubber gloves while giving all manicures
   b. avoid touching the nail after the acrylic primer is applied
   c. sterilize the nailbed with alcohol or peroxide
   d. tell the client to avoid handwashing for 48 hours after nail sculpturing

47. Filing into the corners of your client's toenails can result in
   a. faster nail growth.
   b. ingrown toenails.
   c. corns.
   d. bunions.

48. In massage therapy, a light, continuous stroking movement is
   a. petrissage.
   b. friction.
   c. effleurage.
   d. percussion.

49. Massage benefits the skin and the underlying structures because its general effect is to
   a. speed up the digestive process.
   b. make the client feel sleepy.
   c. stimulate bodily activity in the region
   d. increase sensitivity to pain and fatigue.

50. Facial treatments can have all of the following benefits EXCEPT
   a. increasing the client's self-confidence.
   b. maintaining muscle tone.
   c. preventing break outs.
   d. curing skin cancer.

51. When is infrared light given during a facial?
   a. before facial cleansing
   b. before facial steaming
   c. during or after facial massage
   d. during or after facial cleansing

52. You have used only half of a mask product that comes packaged for one-time use. You should
   a. use the other half for the next client.
   b. discard the remaining product.
   c. sell the remaining product.
   d. take the remainder home for your own use.

53. UV rays are applied with a lamp at what distance from the client?
  a. 10 to 16 inches
  b. 20 to 26 inches
  c. 30 to 36 inches
  d. 40 to 46 inches

54. Face powder serves all of the following functions EXCEPT to
  a. act as a sunscreen.
  b. conceal minor blemishes.
  c. decrease shine.
  d. help to set the makeup in place.

55. Extensions should be attached at what distance from the front hairline, sides, and nape?
  a. 4″
  b. 3″
  c. 2″
  d. 1″

56. In which method are hair extensions secured at the base of the client's own hair by sewing?
  a. sew and cut method
  b. track and knot method
  c. track and sew method
  d. cut and track method

57. Semipermanent individual eyelashes (also called eye tabbing) last approximately
  a. 1 week.
  b. 2–4 weeks.
  c. 4–6 weeks.
  d. 6–8 weeks.

58. The most important technique for the electrologist to master is
  a. timing the pedal depressions.
  b. inserting the needle.
  c. sterilizing the needle.
  d. using the tweezers.

59. What type of hair responds best to laser treatment?
  a. blond, fine hair
  b. coarse, dark hair
  c. red, wiry hair
  d. silver, soft hair

60. The purpose of the neutralizers used in permanent waving is to
  a. break down the hair's structure.
  b. reduce the amount of heat needed.
  c. create a very tight curl.
  d. reharden the hair and fix it into a curl.

61. The purpose of pre-perm shampooing is to
  a. thoroughly wet the hair.
  b. remove residues that might prevent the waving lotion from penetrating.
  c. remove all chemicals that might neutralize the waving lotion.
  d. soften the outer keratin coating.

62. What type of hair texture does a client with fragile, easy to process, easier to damage hair have?
  a. resistant
  b. normal
  c. limp
  d. coarse

63. The most important safety precaution to use when perming a client's hair is to
  a. dilute the chemicals to half strength.
  b. use all chemicals within six months of opening them.
  c. wait three weeks before attempting a second perm on a client who has had an allergic reaction.
  d. read and follow all product directions carefully.

64. To give a client a partial perm, you would
  a. leave the lotion on for half the normal time.
  b. do only the section of the head desired by the client.
  c. wind the rods up only part way.
  d. use very large rods.

65. The purpose of a strand test is to determine
  a. whether any pretreatment is needed.
  b. whether the client is allergic to the tint.
  c. how the final result will look.
  d. how the chosen tint looks in artificial light.

66. Your client complains about her "brassy" haircolor. To neutralize her unwanted highlights, you should use a product that contains
  a. orange.
  b. red.
  c. black.
  d. blue.

67. Which of the following is an example of a natural coloring agent?
  a. metallic hair dye
  b. compound dye
  c. henna
  d. peroxide

68. The purpose of a finishing rinse after coloring hair with a lightener and toner is to close the cuticle and to
  a. stop the lightening process.
  b. achieve the desired color.
  c. adjust the hair's pH.
  d. add blonde highlights.

69. The correct procedure for applying a presoftener is to process for
  a. 2–5 minutes at room temperature.
  b. 5–20 minutes at room temperature.
  c. 2–5 minutes with heat.
  d. 5–20 minutes with heat.

70. When a colorist refers to a contributing pigment, he or she means the
  a. client's natural hair color and tone.
  b. client's desired hair color and tone.
  c. combination of tints that make up the color product.
  d. semipermanent hair color that is added last.

71. When working with aniline-derived products, you should protect yourself from allergic reactions by wearing
  a. goggles.
  b. a face mask.
  c. gloves.
  d. a disposable gown.

72. The relative strength of warm or cool tones in the hair is referred to as
  a. tone.
  b. intensity.
  c. depth.
  d. highlighting.

73. Secondary colors are created by mixing
  a. a primary and a secondary color.
  b. two primary colors in equal proportion.
  c. all three primary colors in equal proportion.
  d. a primary and a tertiary color in equal proportion.

74. Which statement about the effect of henna on the hair is correct?
    a. Henna can be used to obtain bright red shades only.
    b. Henna makes conditioners penetrate the hair more easily.
    c. Henna can make fine hair appear more thick and lustrous.
    d. Henna does not penetrate the hair's cortex layer.

75. A pastel color that is applied only after prelightening is a
    a. tint.
    b. toner.
    c. solvent.
    d. stabilizer.

76. A technique that is particularly useful in avoiding fading in violet-based red hair colors is to
    a. use a low-volume hydrogen peroxide solution.
    b. avoid using hydrogen peroxide.
    c. use a high-volume hydrogen peroxide solution.
    d. apply high heat to the hair during processing.

77. The three steps in chemical hair relaxing are
    a. lather, rinse, repeat.
    b. apply, wait, remove.
    c. presoften, condition, neutralize.
    d. process, neutralize, condition.

78. You should rinse the relaxer out of your client's hair with water that is
    a. cold.
    b. between cool and tepid.
    c. warm.
    d. very hot.

79. The term blunt cutting means
    a. cutting all hair on the head to the same length.
    b. cutting a strand of hair straight across.
    c. slithering.
    d. layering.

80. When you cut the hair at an elevation of below 90 degrees, you are
    a. removing weight.
    b. building weight.
    c. removing bulk.
    d. thinning hair.

81. Name the types of guidelines used in cutting.
    a. stationary and traveling
    b. traveling and returning
    c. stationary and returning
    d. traveling and inactive

82. A point on the head that marks where the surface of the head changes or the behavior of the hair changes is called
    a. a reference point.
    b. a cutting point.
    c. a guiding point.
    d. a scissor point.

83. Combing the hair away from its natural falling position, rather than straight out from the head and cutting it toward a guideline to create a length increase in the design is called
    a. undercutting.
    b. over cutting.
    c. under direction.
    d. over direction.

84. When determining the number of individual hair strands on one square inch of scalp and describing it as thin, medium, or thick is identifying the hair's
a. perimeter.
b. volume.
c. elasticity.
d. density.

85. What is hair texture?
a. the amount of movement in the hair
b. the general quality and feel of the hair
c. the amount of water the hair can absorb
d. the length that the hair can stretch

86. What is wave pattern?
a. the amount of movement in the hair
b. the general quality and feel of the hair
c. the amount of water the hair can absorb
d. the length that the hair can stretch

87. To create short tapers, short haircuts, fades, and flat top styles, which of the following tools is best used?
a. thinning shears
b. edgers
c. straight razor
d. clippers

88. The hair's cortex contains the natural pigment which determines natural haircolor. This pigment is called
a. melatonin.
b. keratin.
c. melanin.
d. keratonin.

89. The purpose of all-over layering of long hair is to
a. thin the hair and make it look neater.
b. add volume and bounce.
c. eliminate split ends.
d. make the hair less curly.

90. A hairstyle for a client with a pear-shaped face should be
a. long and narrow.
b. wide on top.
c. full and high.
d. asymmetrical.

91. If a client asks for an artificial covering for the head consisting of a network of interwoven hair that completely conceals her natural hair, she asking for a
a. braid.
b. wig.
c. fall.
d. weave.

92. The comb used with a thermal iron should be made of
a. hard rubber and have fine teeth.
b. plastic and have fine teeth.
c. bone and have fine teeth.
d. plastic and have coarse teeth.

93. Which type of curl has only slight lift or volume?
a. volume-base curl
b. full-base curl
c. half-base curl
d. off-base curl

94. When giving a thermal setting, after completing each curl, you should
  a. comb it out loosely.
  b. apply clear lacquer.
  c. apply setting gel or lotion.
  d. clip it to its base.

95. During blow drying, hot air is directed
  a. from the scalp toward the hair ends.
  b. straight toward the scalp.
  c. upward from the back of the neck.
  d. downward at all times.

96. Which type of hair requires the least heat and pressure for thermal straightening?
  a. wiry hair
  b. fine hair
  c. medium hair
  d. coarse hair

97. A head-shaped form usually made of canvas-covered cork or Styrofoam, to which the wig is secured for fitting, cleaning, coloring, and styling is called a
  a. round.
  b. mannequin.
  c. block.
  d. square.

98. The advantage of the no-cap wig is that it is
  a. cheaper than other wigs.
  b. made of human hair.
  c. less stretchy than other wigs.
  d. lighter than other wigs.

99. After cleaning a synthetic wig, you should
  a. condition, set, and style it as desired.
  b. hang it up to dry in the sun.
  c. block it and dry it with a hot hair dryer.
  d. block it and allow it to dry naturally.

100. A bandeau is a hairpiece that is
  a. attached to a headband.
  b. attached to a flat base.
  c. secured with an elastic band.
  d. braided and fixed to a wire.

▶ Answers

1. b. If uniforms are not required, you should wear stylish clothing that is neat and reflects the image of the salon.

2. c. Harmful substances include tobacco, illegal drugs, and alcohol.

3. c. An important part of effective communication skills for a cosmetologist is to understand the client's wishes.

4. b. Some clients like to talk; others prefer to be silent. Adapt your behavior to the client's preferences.

5. d. Staphylococci cause skin infections such as abscesses and boils.

6. b. Colds are caused by extremely tiny viruses.

7. b. Personal hygiene and basic sanitation techniques can prevent the spread of infection in the salon.

8. a. A virus lives only by penetrating cells and becoming part of them, while bacteria are organisms that can live on their own.

9. c. Hospital-level disinfectants kill bacteria and fungi only.

10. c. Bleach has been replaced by more modern disinfectants, such as quats.

11. b. Ultrasonic cleaners may be used as an addition to the disinfection process, although ordinary disinfectants are very effective.

12. d. The follicle is the depression in the skin or scalp that the hair shaft grows out of.

13. d. The natural direction of hair growth is referred to as the hair stream.

14. a. Porosity refers to the ability of the hair to absorb moisture.

15. c. Alopecia areata is sometimes treated with ultraviolet light.

16. a. The hair shaft extends above the skin surface.

17. c. The eponychium is the part of the cuticle that extends over the base of the nail.

18. c. White spots are usually caused by previous minor injury to the nail bed.

19. b. Injured nails, manifested by furrows or corrugations, require very gentle treatment.

20. a. The position stop is the point where the nail plate meets the tip before it is glued to the nail.

21. b. A fissure is a crack that penetrates into the dermis.

22. a. Herpes simplex is a contagious disease caused by a virus.

23. d. Epithelial tissue, which includes the skin, scalp, and mucous membranes, is the body's protective covering.

24. b. Muscles are stimulated by heat, electric current, light, and massage, but not by cold.

25. b. The fifth cranial nerve is the major sensory nerve of the face.

26. b. The radial and ulnar arteries supply blood to the arm and hand.

27. a. If a circuit breaker trips the circuit again, immediately call an electrician to locate the problem.

28. b. In electrolysis the current is applied with a very fine, needle-shaped electrode that is inserted into each hair follicle.

29. b. The pH of normal hair is approximately 4.5–5.5; in other words, normal human hair is slightly acidic.

30. c. Protein conditioners are designed to enter the hair shaft and repair damage.

31. c. Fillers, which are made of inexpensive protein products, take up the spaces left in the hair after the diffusion of melanin and, thus, correct its porosity.

32. c. Facial treatments fall under two categories: preservative and corrective. A preservative treatment is meant to maintain the health of the facial skin and a corrective treatment is meant to correct facial skin conditions.

33. a. A lease is an agreement between a building owner and a tenant concerning the renting of property.

34. b. You are not likely to be sued for malpractice if you do your job well. Though having malpractice insurance will help protect you if you are sued, it cannot prevent a suit.

35. d. The receptionist should be courteous and friendly and should call clients by name.

36. c. The best way to please the client is to accommodate yourself to her wishes.

37. a. You fold and secure a towel over the gown to protect the client's skin and clothing.

38. b. For dry hair services, such as a comb out, use a neck strip and cape only.

39. a. Select the shampoo based on your client's hair type.

40. c. The safest procedure is to turn on the cold water first and then adjust the hot water.

41. c. The line of demarcation is the visible line that separates colored hair from newly grown hair.

42. d. Habitual use of cream rinses can make the hair heavy and oily, leading to increased shampooing and further hair damage.

43. c. So that the manicure table is always ready for a new client, clean it immediately after you complete a manicure.

44. a. Always discuss with the client what nail shape he or she wants.

45. a. An oil manicure is beneficial for clients who have brittle or ridged nails or dry cuticles.

46. b. Because the primer contains antiseptics to prevent the growth of fungus, avoid touching the nail after you apply the primer.

47. b. File the nails straight across to avoid ingrown toenails.

48. c. Effleurage is a light, continuous stroking movement.

49. c. Massage stimulates all local activity, including circulation, muscle tone, and secretions from skin glands.

50. d. Although facial treatments can benefit clients with some skin conditions, they cannot cure skin cancer.

51. c. Infrared treatment is commonly given during or after facial massage.

52. b. To avoid the risk of contamination, you should always discard disposable supplies after each facial.

53. c. UV rays are applied with a lamp at a distance of 30 to 36 inches and the therapy should begin with exposure times of 2 to 3 minutes with a gradual increase in exposure time to 7 or 8 minutes.

54. a. Face powder does not act as a sunscreen because it does not protect the skin from the harmful rays of the sun.

55. d. No hair extensions should ever be any closer to the front hairline, sides, and nape area than one inch.

56. c. In the track and sew method, hair extensions are secured at the base of the client's own hair by sewing and the hair is attached to an on-the-scalp braid which serves as the track.

57. d. These lashes, which are attached to individual natural lashes, fall out along with the natural lashes and last approximately 6–8 weeks.

58. b. Learning the correct angle and depth at which to insert the needle is critical to learning the proper technique.

59. b. An absolute requirement for using the laser to remove hair is that one's hair must be darker than the surrounding skin. Coarse, dark hair responds best to laser treatment.

60. d. Without neutralizer, the hair shape would revert after one or two shampoos.

61. b. Pre-perm shampooing must remove all residues and coatings that might prevent the waving lotion from penetrating the hair strands.

62. c. Fragile, easy to process, easier to damage hair indicates a client with fine, limp hair texture.

63. a. Always read and follow all product directions carefully.

64. b. A partial perm does only the section of the head desired by the client.

65. c. The purpose of a strand test is to determine how the final result will look.

66. d. Blue, the complementary color to orange, will neutralize unwanted orange tones.

67. c. Henna is a natural, plant-based product.

68. c. The finishing rinse is needed to adjust the hair's acidity because toners are highly alkaline.

69. b. The correct procedure is 5–20 minutes at room temperature.

70. a. The contributing pigment is the client's underlying hair color.

71. c. Wear gloves at all times when working with aniline-derived products.

72. b. The relative strength of the warm or cool tones is intensity.

73. b. Secondary colors are created by mixing two primary colors in equal proportion.

74. c. Because henna coats the surface of the hair, it can make fine hair appear thicker and more lustrous.

75. b. A toner is a pastel hair color that is applied after prelightening.

76. a. Using a low-volume hydrogen peroxide solution can prevent violet-based reds from fading.

77. d. The three basic steps are process, neutralize, condition.

78. c. Cold or cool water will not stop the relaxing process, and very hot water will irritate the client's scalp.

79. b. Blunt cutting means cutting each strand of hair straight across, without slithering.

80. b. You will build weight when you elevate the hair below 90 degrees in a hair cut.

81. a. The two types of guidelines are stationary guides which do not move about the head and traveling guides which are used to ensure that each section in a particular part of the head are cut evenly.

82. a. The reference point marks a surface on the head where the behavior of the hair changes which indicates to the cutter a place where his technique may need to be altered.

83. d. Over direction occurs when you comb the hair away from its natural falling position, rather than straight out from the head, toward a guideline and it is used in graduated and layered haircuts to create a length increase in the design.

84. d. Hair density is the number of individual hair strands on one square inch of scalp and is usually described as thin, medium, or thick.

85. a. Hair texture is the general quality and feel of the hair and is usually classified as coarse, medium, and fine.

86. b. The wave pattern is the amount of movement in the hair strand and is usually classified as stick-straight hair, wavy hair, curly hair, extremely curly hair, or anything in between.

87. d. Electric clippers make creating short tapers, short haircuts, fades, and flat tops easy and efficient.

88. c. The cortex contains the natural pigment called melanin, which determines natural hair-color. There are two types of melanin in the cortex: eumelanin is the melanin that gives black and brown color to hair and pheomelanin is the melanin found in red hair.

89. b. All-over layering adds volume and swing to long hair.

90. c. A high, full style will camouflage the facial shape.

91. b. A wig can be defined as an artificial covering for the head consisting of a network of interwoven hair that completely covers the client's natural hair and is mainly used for covering up hair loss from aging or disease or to temporarily change their look.

92. a. The comb should be made of a nonflammable material, such as hard rubber; fine teeth hold the hair more firmly.

93. d. An off-base curl provides only slight lift or volume.

94. d. Clip each curl to its base until the whole head is completed.

95. a. During blow drying, the hot air is directed from the scalp toward the hair ends, not directly toward the scalp.

96. b. Fine hair requires the least heat and pressure to be thermally straightened.

97. c. A block is a head-shaped form that holds the wig for the entire time the wig is not being worn by its owner and the wig is on the block during fitting, cleaning, coloring, and styling.

98. d. No-cap wigs are lighter and, therefore, more comfortable to wear than other wigs.

99. d. Synthetic wigs should not be exposed to heat, and setting and styling are unnecessary.

100. a. A bandeau is a hairpiece that is attached to a headband, which conceals the hairline.

7 ▶ Cosmetology Practice Exam 4

CHAPTER SUMMARY

This is the last of four practice exams in this book that are based on the core content of your cosmetology coursework. Using all of the experience and strategy that you gained from the other three exams and from the Refresher Course, take this test to guage how much you have learned and retained using this book.

THOUGH THIS IS the last practice exam, it is not designed to be any harder or trickier than the other three. It is simply another representation of what you can expect to find on the official cosmetology exam. There shouldn't be anything here to surprise you. In fact, you probably will feel very comfortable with the exam. That's the idea for the real test, too—you won't be surprised, so you won't be unprepared.

For this last test, pull together all the tips you've been practicing since the first test. Give yourself the time and the space to work—perhaps in an unfamiliar location such as a library, since you won't be taking the official exam in your living room. In addition, draw on what you've learned from reading the answer explanations. Remember the types of questions that tripped you up in the past, and when you are unsure, try to consider how these answers were explained.

Most of all, relax. You have worked hard and have every right to be confident!

The answer sheet is on the following page, followed by the exam. The correct answers, each fully explained, follow the exam. When you have read and understood all the answers, turn back to Chapter 1 for an explanation of how to score and analyze your exam. You will then determine possible weak areas to study further in Chapter 4, the Cosmetology Refresher Course.

Practice Exam 4

1.	ⓐ	ⓑ	ⓒ	ⓓ
2.	ⓐ	ⓑ	ⓒ	ⓓ
3.	ⓐ	ⓑ	ⓒ	ⓓ
4.	ⓐ	ⓑ	ⓒ	ⓓ
5.	ⓐ	ⓑ	ⓒ	ⓓ
6.	ⓐ	ⓑ	ⓒ	ⓓ
7.	ⓐ	ⓑ	ⓒ	ⓓ
8.	ⓐ	ⓑ	ⓒ	ⓓ
9.	ⓐ	ⓑ	ⓒ	ⓓ
10.	ⓐ	ⓑ	ⓒ	ⓓ
11.	ⓐ	ⓑ	ⓒ	ⓓ
12.	ⓐ	ⓑ	ⓒ	ⓓ
13.	ⓐ	ⓑ	ⓒ	ⓓ
14.	ⓐ	ⓑ	ⓒ	ⓓ
15.	ⓐ	ⓑ	ⓒ	ⓓ
16.	ⓐ	ⓑ	ⓒ	ⓓ
17.	ⓐ	ⓑ	ⓒ	ⓓ
18.	ⓐ	ⓑ	ⓒ	ⓓ
19.	ⓐ	ⓑ	ⓒ	ⓓ
20.	ⓐ	ⓑ	ⓒ	ⓓ
21.	ⓐ	ⓑ	ⓒ	ⓓ
22.	ⓐ	ⓑ	ⓒ	ⓓ
23.	ⓐ	ⓑ	ⓒ	ⓓ
24.	ⓐ	ⓑ	ⓒ	ⓓ
25.	ⓐ	ⓑ	ⓒ	ⓓ
26.	ⓐ	ⓑ	ⓒ	ⓓ
27.	ⓐ	ⓑ	ⓒ	ⓓ
28.	ⓐ	ⓑ	ⓒ	ⓓ
29.	ⓐ	ⓑ	ⓒ	ⓓ
30.	ⓐ	ⓑ	ⓒ	ⓓ
31.	ⓐ	ⓑ	ⓒ	ⓓ
32.	ⓐ	ⓑ	ⓒ	ⓓ
33.	ⓐ	ⓑ	ⓒ	ⓓ
34.	ⓐ	ⓑ	ⓒ	ⓓ
35.	ⓐ	ⓑ	ⓒ	ⓓ

36.	ⓐ	ⓑ	ⓒ	ⓓ
37.	ⓐ	ⓑ	ⓒ	ⓓ
38.	ⓐ	ⓑ	ⓒ	ⓓ
39.	ⓐ	ⓑ	ⓒ	ⓓ
40.	ⓐ	ⓑ	ⓒ	ⓓ
41.	ⓐ	ⓑ	ⓒ	ⓓ
42.	ⓐ	ⓑ	ⓒ	ⓓ
43.	ⓐ	ⓑ	ⓒ	ⓓ
44.	ⓐ	ⓑ	ⓒ	ⓓ
45.	ⓐ	ⓑ	ⓒ	ⓓ
46.	ⓐ	ⓑ	ⓒ	ⓓ
47.	ⓐ	ⓑ	ⓒ	ⓓ
48.	ⓐ	ⓑ	ⓒ	ⓓ
49.	ⓐ	ⓑ	ⓒ	ⓓ
50.	ⓐ	ⓑ	ⓒ	ⓓ
51.	ⓐ	ⓑ	ⓒ	ⓓ
52.	ⓐ	ⓑ	ⓒ	ⓓ
53.	ⓐ	ⓑ	ⓒ	ⓓ
54.	ⓐ	ⓑ	ⓒ	ⓓ
55.	ⓐ	ⓑ	ⓒ	ⓓ
56.	ⓐ	ⓑ	ⓒ	ⓓ
57.	ⓐ	ⓑ	ⓒ	ⓓ
58.	ⓐ	ⓑ	ⓒ	ⓓ
59.	ⓐ	ⓑ	ⓒ	ⓓ
60.	ⓐ	ⓑ	ⓒ	ⓓ
61.	ⓐ	ⓑ	ⓒ	ⓓ
62.	ⓐ	ⓑ	ⓒ	ⓓ
63.	ⓐ	ⓑ	ⓒ	ⓓ
64.	ⓐ	ⓑ	ⓒ	ⓓ
65.	ⓐ	ⓑ	ⓒ	ⓓ
66.	ⓐ	ⓑ	ⓒ	ⓓ
67.	ⓐ	ⓑ	ⓒ	ⓓ
68.	ⓐ	ⓑ	ⓒ	ⓓ
69.	ⓐ	ⓑ	ⓒ	ⓓ
70.	ⓐ	ⓑ	ⓒ	ⓓ

71.	ⓐ	ⓑ	ⓒ	ⓓ
72.	ⓐ	ⓑ	ⓒ	ⓓ
73.	ⓐ	ⓑ	ⓒ	ⓓ
74.	ⓐ	ⓑ	ⓒ	ⓓ
75.	ⓐ	ⓑ	ⓒ	ⓓ
76.	ⓐ	ⓑ	ⓒ	ⓓ
77.	ⓐ	ⓑ	ⓒ	ⓓ
78.	ⓐ	ⓑ	ⓒ	ⓓ
79.	ⓐ	ⓑ	ⓒ	ⓓ
80.	ⓐ	ⓑ	ⓒ	ⓓ
81.	ⓐ	ⓑ	ⓒ	ⓓ
82.	ⓐ	ⓑ	ⓒ	ⓓ
83.	ⓐ	ⓑ	ⓒ	ⓓ
84.	ⓐ	ⓑ	ⓒ	ⓓ
85.	ⓐ	ⓑ	ⓒ	ⓓ
86.	ⓐ	ⓑ	ⓒ	ⓓ
87.	ⓐ	ⓑ	ⓒ	ⓓ
88.	ⓐ	ⓑ	ⓒ	ⓓ
89.	ⓐ	ⓑ	ⓒ	ⓓ
90.	ⓐ	ⓑ	ⓒ	ⓓ
91.	ⓐ	ⓑ	ⓒ	ⓓ
92.	ⓐ	ⓑ	ⓒ	ⓓ
93.	ⓐ	ⓑ	ⓒ	ⓓ
94.	ⓐ	ⓑ	ⓒ	ⓓ
95.	ⓐ	ⓑ	ⓒ	ⓓ
96.	ⓐ	ⓑ	ⓒ	ⓓ
97.	ⓐ	ⓑ	ⓒ	ⓓ
98.	ⓐ	ⓑ	ⓒ	ⓓ
99.	ⓐ	ⓑ	ⓒ	ⓓ
100.	ⓐ	ⓑ	ⓒ	ⓓ

▶ Practice Exam 4

1. Your client asks you if she should use a hair rinse. The most professional reply would be
   a. "Yes—your hair really needs help."
   b. "I don't know anything about it."
   c. "Many of our clients find that this rinse makes their hair shinier."
   d. "Definitely—I've been noticing that your hair is getting more brittle all the time."

2. Good posture is important to cosmetologists both to improve personal appearance as well as to
   a. command a higher salary.
   b. prevent fatigue and physical problems.
   c. increase self-confidence.
   d. promote and strengthen self-discipline.

3. You have just finished styling a client's hair, and she angrily demands a "different look." What should you say?
   a. "This is what you told me to do!"
   b. "Can you explain what you want?"
   c. "Your hair really looks so much better now!"
   d. "Do you want to come back tomorrow?"

4. As a cosmetologist, you would be acting professionally if you
   a. called all clients by their first names when you first met them.
   b. discussed your coworkers' work skills with clients.
   c. demonstrated a pleasant personality and friendly attitude.
   d. always talked about your own problems with clients.

5. Short, rod-shaped bacteria are referred to as
   a. bacilli.
   b. cocci.
   c. spirilla.
   d. streptococci.

6. Scabies is caused by a
   a. virus.
   b. bacteria.
   c. louse.
   d. mite.

7. AIDS can be spread in all of the following ways EXCEPT
   a. sexual intercourse.
   b. sharing needles.
   c. blood transfusions.
   d. shaking hands.

8. An important rule of sanitation is to
   a. reuse client gowns or headbands only three times before washing.
   b. wash your hands after using the restroom and between clients.
   c. store pins, rollers, and other tools in your pockets.
   d. make sure clients' pets are kept near them and not allowed to roam freely.

9. A client has an open sore on her scalp. You should work on her hair only if
   a. her doctor certifies that it is not infectious.
   b. she assures you that it is safe.
   c. you cover the sore with a bandage.
   d. she insists that she cannot come back another day.

10. For hand-washing, salons should provide
  a. disinfectants.
  b. liquid antiseptic soaps.
  c. antibacterial bar soaps.
  d. formalin.

11. Which statement about the use of formalin in dry cabinet sanitizers is correct?
  a. Formalin must be used in a 100% concentration.
  b. Formalin should be used in place of formaldehyde.
  c. Formalin releases a carcinogen and should not be used.
  d. Formalin has been replaced by quats.

12. Sebaceous glands in the scalp and skin produce
  a. sweat.
  b. dandruff.
  c. oil.
  d. keratin.

13. Which of the following factors does **NOT** affect the general health of a person's hair?
  a. diet
  b. physical health
  c. emotional state
  d. weather

14. The hair's pigment, or color, is found in its
  a. epidermis.
  b. cortex.
  c. medulla.
  d. cuticle.

15. Which statement about dandruff is correct?
  a. Any client with dandruff requires medical treatment.
  b. Both kinds of dandruff are considered to be contagious.
  c. The waxy type of dandruff can be treated with hot oil treatments.
  d. Dandruff is caused by poor personal hygiene.

16. Hair is made of the same protein as the
  a. teeth.
  b. bones.
  c. nails.
  d. muscles.

17. The average nail grows approximately how fast?
  a. 1/8 inch per week
  b. 1/4 inch per week
  c. 1/8 inch per month
  d 1/4 inch per month

18. Light-cured and no-light cured are types of what kind of nail overlay?
  a. powder
  b. fabric
  c. adhesive
  d. gels

19. Your client has severely bitten nails and asks for advice on stopping this habit. You should advise him or her that
  a. most people are unable to stop.
  b. frequent manicures may motivate him or her to stop.
  c. placing bad-tasting powders on the nails can be effective.
  d. this habit is hereditary.

20. The main effect of aging on the skin is
a. loss of elasticity.
b. increased amount of subcutaneous tissue.
c. increased blood flow.
d. loss of hair follicles.

21. Which of the following is an example of a seasonal condition?
a. acne
b. rosacea
c. herpes simplex
d. prickly heat

22. A callus that grows inward is referred to as a
a. cyst.
b. corn.
c. mole.
d. sarcoma.

23. The integumentary system includes the
a. skin and its accessory organs.
b. bones and muscles.
c. heart, lungs, and blood vessels.
d. digestive organs and glands.

24. As a cosmetologist, you need to understand the muscle structure of the face and neck in order to
a. avoid hurting your clients during chemical treatments.
b. choose the most attractive hair colors.
c. give an effective and relaxing massage.
d. apply makeup most effectively.

25. Which branch of the seventh cranial nerve affects the muscles at the base of the skull behind the ear?
a. temporal
b. infraorbital
c. posterior auricular
d. supratrochlear

26. The sweat and oil glands found in the skin are examples of
a. lymphatic ducts.
b. endocrine glands.
c. ductless glands.
d. exocrine glands.

27. While using high-frequency current, the client should avoid contact with
a. cloth gowns.
b. metal chair arms.
c. vinyl seats.
d. rubber gloves.

28. A primary benefit of infrared treatment to the skin is to
a. cool the body by increasing perspiration.
b. slow the metabolism and cause relaxation.
c. decrease the skin's production of sweat and oil.
d. dilate blood vessels and increase circulation.

29. Which of the following hair-care substances has an acidic pH?
a. conditioner
b. semipermanent color
c. cold waving lotion
d. hair relaxer

30. Permanent waving works by
a. breaking and rearranging the hair's disulfide bonds.
b. stretching and reconfiguring the hair's H and S bonds.
c. coating the hair shaft with strong protein molecules.
d. completely severing the hair's disulfide bonds.

31. Which substance is capable of dissolving the greatest number of other substances?
   a. water
   b. oil
   c. alcohol
   d. glycerin

32. Which of these is **NOT** an advantage of booth renting?
   a. You can own your own business for a small investment.
   b. You can control the type and amount of products you use.
   c. All of your overhead expenses are low.
   d. You can call in sick and know that your clients will be taken care of by another stylist.

33. A complete business plan would include all of the following **EXCEPT**
   a. a description of the proposed business.
   b. a profit and loss statement.
   c. the names and addresses of employees.
   d. the number of employees and total salaries.

34. The largest expense involved in running a salon is for
   a. insurance.
   b. advertising.
   c. salaries.
   d. supplies.

35. The primary goal of scheduling appointments is to ensure that
   a. all salon workers' time is used efficiently.
   b. clients never wait longer than half an hour.
   c. cosmetologists earn the maximum in tips.
   d. the receptionist is kept busy at all times.

36. When styling the hair of an elderly client, you should be sure to
   a. suggest a youthful hairstyle.
   b. be helpful and courteous.
   c. talk as little as possible.
   d. play soft background music.

37. After shampooing a client, what additional step is necessary to prepare her for a haircut?
   a. Remove the drape and both towels.
   b. Remove the outer towel and replace it with a neck strip.
   c. Fold and secure a third towel over the drape.
   d. Remove the neck strip and replace it with a second towel.

38. Before draping a client, you should ask her to remove her jewelry and
   a. give it to you for safekeeping.
   b. leave it at the front desk.
   c. put it away in a safe place.
   d. take it home for safekeeping.

39. The reflective listening technique is used
   a. when you talk to a client in the mirror.
   b. to prove you see the client clearly.
   c. when the client responds to you in the mirror.
   d. to prove that you have heard and understand your client.

40. How should a stylist approach selling additional products and services to clients?
   a. knowing the additional commission she will make
   b. with a smooth line about the benefits of the additional sale
   c. with sincere concern for the client's needs
   d. with disregard for whether or not the client needs the product or service

41. The correct way to manipulate the scalp during a shampoo is to start at the
   a. nape of the neck.
   b. top of the head.
   c. sides of the head.
   d. front hairline.

42. A shampoo with a pH higher than 7.0 is said to be
   a. mild
   b. for dry hair
   c. acid
   d. alkaline

43. The main effect of occasional use of a cream rinse is to
   a. make the hair softer and easier to comb.
   b. prevent shampoo buildup on the scalp.
   c. correct the pH of the hair and scalp.
   d. eliminate minor dandruff problems.

44. During a manicure, you should place all waste materials in
   a. your pocket.
   b. a central laundry receptacle for dirty linen.
   c. a plastic bag attached to the manicure table.
   d. the drawer of the manicure table.

45. It is important to use light pressure when working with a cuticle pusher or orangewood stick so that the
   a. tools will not be bent or damaged.
   b. nailbed will not be injured.
   c. nail tip will not weaken and break.
   d. nail polish will not be accidentally removed.

46. The purpose of nail wrapping is to
   a. make the nails grow longer.
   b. provide a base coat for nail polish.
   c. provide an interesting texture to the nail.
   d. strengthen nails or mend a broken nail.

47. When applying press-on artificial nails, you should put the adhesive on the
   a. underside of the client's nails.
   b. inside of the artificial nails only.
   c. center of the client's nails and inside of the artificial nails.
   d. edges of the client's nails and inside of the artificial nails.

48. When giving a pedicure, you should loosen and push back the cuticles with
   a. a metal pusher.
   b. your fingers.
   c. an orangewood stick.
   d. a cotton swab.

49. A deep, rubbing movement is referred to as
   a. petrissage.
   b. friction.
   c. effleurage.
   d. percussion.

50. A normal skin and scalp can obtain the greatest benefit from a massage once each
   a. day.
   b. week.
   c. month.
   d. year.

51. You should help your client to relax before a facial by
   a. explaining your sanitary procedures in detail
   b. providing a pleasant, quiet atmosphere and speaking professionally
   c. providing printed literature on the benefits of facial treatments
   d. describing your training and experience in detail

52. The correct order for a facial is
   a. mask, steaming, massage, cleansing.
   b. cleansing, steaming, massage, mask.
   c. cleansing, massage, steaming, mask.
   d. cleansing, mask, steaming, massage.

53. Your client has acne, and some of the pimples have come to a head and are open. You should
   a. wear rubber gloves while working on the client.
   b. refuse to give a facial while the condition is active.
   c. use only nondisposable materials for the client.
   d. give a facial only under a doctor's specific orders.

54. The correct procedure for applying gauze for a facial mask is to
   a. apply the gauze to the face, then add the mask ingredients.
   b. mix the gauze with the mask ingredients before applying to the face.
   c. apply the ingredients to the face, then cover with gauze.
   d. apply three layers of gauze to the face, add the mask ingredients, and cover with three more layers.

55. When a client prefers to wear a very dark or bright lip color, you should choose a cheek color that is
   a. brighter.
   b. darker.
   c. lighter.
   d. the same.

56. When applying makeup on a client, your goal should be to
   a. promote the products your salon sells.
   b. make the client look like a favorite movie star.
   c. make the client look as if she has no bad features.
   d. minimize the bad features and maximize the good ones.

57. To correct a long, thin neck, you should apply a lighter shade of foundation
   a. on the face than on the neck.
   b. at the front of the face only.
   c. on the neck than on the face.
   d. at the sides of the neck only.

58. When applying semipermanent individual eyelashes (eye tabbing), a right-handed cosmetologist would start working on the upper lid at the
   a. inner corner of the left eye.
   b. outer corner of the left eye.
   c. inner corner of the right eye.
   d. outer corner of the right eye.

59. The correct procedure for thermolysis is to start with low current and to increase the intensity and time until the
   a. test hair comes out easily.
   b. client feels a slight shock.
   c. client can no longer stand the pain.
   d. maximum dose is reached.

60. When using hot wax, you should test the temperature by
   a. inserting the tip of a fever thermometer into the container.
   b. spreading a small amount of wax on your arm.
   c. asking the client to put her hand into the container.
   d. putting your hand into the container.

61. An important first step that helps ensure that your client will be satisfied with a permanent is to
   a. show the client how you think she should look.
   b. tell the client how experienced you are at doing perms.
   c. discuss the client's expectations and lifestyle.
   d. be familiar with the latest, most fashionable hairstyles.

62. Concave rods will create a curl that is
   a. the same size throughout its length.
   b. tighter at the top than at the ends.
   c. tighter at the ends than at the top.
   d. extremely loose throughout.

63. During the client consultation which of following is **NOT** a tool you should prepare for use with the client?
   a. styling books
   b. hair swatches
   c. mannequins
   d. color mixing bowl

64. The length of time you should spend rinsing the lotion out of the hair depends on the
   a. texture of the hair.
   b. size of the rods.
   c. manufacturer's instructions.
   d. tightness of the curls desired.

65. Hair can be permed successfully if it has been
   a. severely damaged.
   b. treated with a sodium hydroxide hair relaxer.
   c. treated with henna hair color.
   d. tinted or bleached.

66. Very long hair can present a challenge for the colorist because the ends of the hair are
   a. dark.
   b. overporous.
   c. coarse.
   d. extremely dense.

67. Color shampoos may be used to add slight color to the hair, to brighten the color, or to
   a. bleach away natural color.
   b. permanently eliminate gray hair.
   c. cover unwanted color tones.
   d. preview the results of haircoloring.

68. A professional cosmetologist must be able to recognize when a client has used metallic or compound dyes because
   a. the colors achieved cannot be duplicated at home.
   b. these products conflict with professional hair-care products.
   c. hair treated with these products can only be lightened with concentrated hydrogen peroxide.
   d. these products are illegal to buy or use.

69. You are using the cap technique for highlighting. To achieve a subtle effect, you would
   a. apply very small pieces of foil.
   b. use small amounts of toner.
   c. lighten only the hair under the cap.
   d. pull out only a few small strands.

70. The purpose of a filler is to correct the hair's porosity and to
    a. cleanse the hair ends.
    b. deposit a base color.
    c. deep condition the hair shafts.
    d. remove unwanted red tones.

71. Neutralization is a process that
    a. speeds up a chemical reaction.
    b. stops a chemical reaction.
    c. removes heat from a chemical process.
    d. adds acid to a chemical reaction.

72. If a skin test is positive, the client will report
    a. redness or burning.
    b. a severe headache.
    c. chest pain.
    d. swollen feet and legs.

73. When formulating a color for gray hair, it is important to consider the
    a. client's natural hair color before turning gray.
    b. particular shade of gray in the client's hair.
    c. length and condition of the client's hair.
    d. price the client is willing to pay for hair coloring.

74. Which color neutralizes a too-orange color?
    a. blue
    b. violet
    c. green
    d. brown

75. Which type of hair color product can lighten and deposit color in a single step?
    a. semipermanent hair colors
    b. natural henna products
    c. hydrogen peroxide
    d. oxidative hair color

76. After lightening, each individual hair shaft will become
    a. coarser and more pliable.
    b. coarser and less pliable.
    c. less coarse and more pliable.
    d. less coarse and less pliable.

77. Your client has brown hair that is 20% gray. To achieve a natural-looking all-over hair color, you should use a permanent color formulation that is
    a. one level lighter than desired.
    b. equal parts of the desired level and one level lighter.
    c. the same as the desired level.
    d. one level darker than desired.

78. The main purpose of keeping a written record of a client's hair relaxing treatments is to
    a. ensure consistent and satisfactory future results.
    b. protect the cosmetologist and salon from legal liability.
    c. learn more about the chemical reaction involved.
    d. learn how to increase the strength of the reaction.

79. If rinse water gets into your client's eyes after a chemical hair relaxing treatment, you should
    a. rinse the eyes and refer the client to a doctor.
    b. call for an ambulance immediately.
    c. rinse the eyes with cold water.
    d. call your supervisor immediately to examine the eyes.

80. Clients who receive regular facial treatments can expect them to help
   a. decrease circulation.
   b. deactivate glandular activity.
   c. relax the nerves.
   d. corrode muscle tone.

81. In haircutting, the first step in four-section parting is to part the hair
   a. from ear to ear.
   b. from the forehead to the nape.
   c. across the crown.
   d. vertically above each ear.

82. You should **NOT** thin a client's hair
   a. at the top of the head.
   b. if it is very curly.
   c. if it has been tinted.
   d. near the hairline.

83. What factor plays a major role in guiding you to the desired end result in haircutting?
   a. the cutting guide
   b. the head form
   c. the hair texture
   d. the scissor shape

84. Top and crown layering of long hair prevents the hair from
   a. becoming frizzy in humid weather.
   b. developing split ends.
   c. becoming oily.
   d. lying too close to the head.

85. Which of these is **NOT** a texture service?
   a. permanent waving
   b. finger waving
   c. soft curl permanents
   d. chemical hair relaxing

86. A shadow wave is a
   a. shallow wave with low ridges.
   b. finger wave that is beneath another wave.
   c. wave at the back of the head.
   d. wave at the nape of the neck.

87. At what temperature does an acid wave process at?
   a. heated temperature
   b. room temperature
   c. freezing temperature
   d. below zero temperature

88. What type of perm creates a chemical reaction that heats up the perming solution and speeds up the processing?
   a. acid balanced
   b. endothermic
   c. apple pectin
   d. exothermic

89. What is the relationship between roller size and the resulting curl?
   a. The smaller the roller, the tighter the curl.
   b. The larger the roller, the tighter the curl.
   c. There is no relationship.
   d. The relationship depends more on direction of roll than on size.

90. Which hairstyle would be most flattering for a client with a prominent nose?
   a. a swept-back hairstyle
   b. an upswept hairstyle
   c. a tight, pulled-back bun or french twist
   d. a forward hairstyle with softness around the face

91. In designing a hairstyle for a client with very thin features, you should aim to
a. create an asymmetrical effect.
b. add width to the face and neck.
c. cover the face as much as possible.
d. add as much length as possible.

92. Before beginning a thermal wave, you should.
a. apply setting lotion.
b. back-comb the section of hair to be waved.
c. comb the hair in the direction of the wave.
d. thoroughly wet the strand of hair.

93. To form a half-base curl, you would hold the hair at an angle of
a. 135 degrees.
b. 125 degrees.
c. 90 degrees.
d. 70 degrees.

94. You should **NOT** use vaporizing irons on hair that has been
a. thinned and cut short.
b. pressed.
c. previously blown dry.
d. set.

95. To give the crown hair a lift during blow drying, you would use
a. a round brush.
b. a vent brush.
c. a very large diameter brush.
d. an air waver with comb attachment.

96. To clean a pressing comb before and after each use, you should
a. use antiseptic.
b. place it in a sterilizer.
c. wash it with soap and hot water.
d. wipe it clean.

97. Pressing hair that is incompletely dried can result in
a. drying.
b. burning or smoking.
c. cracking or peeling.
d. splitting.

98. To fit a wig properly, you would measure the circumference of the head by placing the tape measure
a. at the forehead hairline and going all the way around the head just above the ears.
b. at the nape of the neck and extending up to the forehead hairline.
c. above the eyebrows and going all the way around the head.
d. two inches above one ear and extending all the way around the head at that level.

99. If a lock is totally closed at the end and the hair is tightly meshed, what stage is the braid in?
a. pre-lock stage
b. sprouting stage
c. growing stage
d. maturation stage

100. A knot or coil of synthetic hair is referred to as a
a. chignon.
b. braid.
c. fall.
d. bandeau.

► Answers

1. c. This reply is tactful and professional and may be successful in selling a new product to the client.

2. b. Good posture improves physical appearance as well as preventing fatigue and physical problems.

3. b. When a client becomes angry or hostile, ask open-ended questions to determine what the problem is.

4. c. Your personality and attitude toward your job and your clients are parts of professionalism.

5. a. Short, rod-shaped bacteria are known as bacilli.

6. d. Scabies is caused by a tiny mite that burrows beneath the skin.

7. d. AIDS cannot be spread by ordinary social contact, such as shaking hands or kissing.

8. b. Always wash your hands between clients and after using the restroom.

9. a. You should not work on a client with an open sore unless a doctor certifies that it is not infectious.

10. b. Because bacteria can grow on bar soaps, liquid antiseptic soaps are the safest for hand-washing.

11. c. Formalin releases formaldehyde, a known carcinogen, and should not be used in the salon.

12. c. Sebaceous glands are the oil-producing glands in the skin and scalp.

13. d. A person's diet, state of physical and emotional health, and any drugs he or she takes can influence the health of the hair.

14. b. The hair's pigmented layer is the middle layer, or cortex.

15. b. Both dry and waxy dandruff are considered to be contagious conditions.

16. c. Hair is composed of the protein keratin, the same protein that is found in the nails and skin.

17. c. The average nail grows approximately 1/8 inch per month.

18. c. Adhesive or dipped nails are reliant on a cyanoacrylate, a very fast-setting glue which comes in different viscosities and can be applied in several ways.

19. b. Frequent manicures are sometimes effective in helping people to stop biting their nails.

20. a. The loss of elasticity that occurs with age is the main cause of wrinkling and sagging.

21. d. A seasonal condition is triggered at particular seasons of the year, such as prickly heat, which appears in hot weather.

22. b. A corn is a callus that grows inward and becomes painful.

23. a. The integumentary system is made up of the skin and the oil glands, sweat glands, hair, and nails.

24. c. An understanding of the muscles of the head, face, and neck will allow you to give an effective massage.

25. c. The posterior auricular nerve gives motor function to these muscles.

26. d. The exocrine, or duct glands, have canals for transporting the product of the gland to a particular part of the body.

27. b. Touching metal while in contact with the electrode will cause a short circuit and result in a serious burn.

28. d. Infrared light can dilate peripheral blood vessels, increasing circulation to the skin.

29. a. Most other hair-care substances are alkaline.

30. a. Permanent waving works by breaking and then rearranging the disulfide bonds (straightening breaks them without reconnecting them).

31. a. Because of its ability to dissolve so many other substances, water is referred to as the universal solvent.

32. d. The advantages of booth renting are that you can become your own boss for a small amount of money, your initial investment is also small, and expenses are generally low but you have only yourself to rely on for handling your customers.

33. c. A business plan is a financial plan that you develop before you open a business.

34. c. Salaries are by far the largest expense involved in running a salon.

35. a. Careful scheduling will ensure that neither the client nor the cosmetologist is kept waiting.

36. b. Be especially courteous to elderly clients, and offer any special help they may need.

37. b. Replace the outer towel with a neck strip before cutting the hair.

38. c. The client should put his or her jewelry away in a safe place.

39. d. The reflective listening technique is used to prove that you have heard and understand your client. In reflective listening, you will repeat in your own words what you believe your client just told you. This will determine whether the two of you are on the same page or not.

40. c. A stylist should approach selling to clients with sincere concern for their needs and by recommending only what is truly in the client's best interest.

41. d. Begin at the front hairline and work your way down.

42. d. A pH higher than 7.0 is alkaline; the higher the pH, the harsher the shampoo.

43. a. Cream rinses and conditioners can make the hair softer and easier to comb.

44. c. There should always be a small plastic bag hanging from the side of the manicure table to hold waste materials.

45. b. Too much pressure on the cuticle can injure the nailbed.

46. d. Nail wrapping is done to strengthen weak nails or to mend broken ones.

47. d. Apply adhesive sparingly to the inside of the artificial nails and to the edges of the client's nails.

48. c. Use an orangewood stick to gently push back the cuticles.

49. b. Friction is a deep rubbing movement.

50. b. Weekly massage provides the greatest benefit to the normal skin and scalp.

51. b. A pleasant, quiet atmosphere and a professional manner will help the client relax.

52. b. This answer choice gives the correct order of steps in giving a facial.

53. a. Wear rubber gloves and use disposable materials while working on a client with this kind of acne.

54. a. The correct procedure is given in this answer choice. Sometimes a second layer of gauze is placed above the mask ingredients.

55. c. When a client wears a very dark or bright lip color, choose a lighter coordinating cheek color.

56. d. Your goal is to make the client look her best.

57. c. Apply a lighter shade of foundation on the entire neck to create an illusion of fullness.

58. b. The procedure given in this answer choice is the easiest to follow.

59. a. Increase the intensity and time gradually until a test hair comes out easily.

60. b. Spread some wax on your arm to test the temperature and consistency.

61. c. Clients will be most satisfied if the final results meet their expectations and fit their lifestyle.

62. c. Concave rods will create a curl that is tighter at the ends.

63. d. It is not necessary to have a color mixing bowl during the client consultation.

64. c. The instructions will tell you exactly how long to rinse the lotion from the hair.

65. d. Hair that has been tinted or bleached can usually be permed successfully if you choose the right waving formula.

66. b. The ends of long hair may be overporous and may, therefore, accept color differently than the rest of the hair.

67. c. Color shampoos can cover unwanted tones, in addition to brightening the hair.

68. b. These products, which are used in the home but not in the salon, can cause adverse chemical reactions with most professional products.

69. d. To achieve a subtle effect, pull out and lighten only a few small strands.

70. b. A filler will correct the hair's porosity and deposit a base color.

71. b. To neutralize a reaction or a process means to stop it.

72. a. Redness, burning, itching, or blisters at the site are indications of a positive skin text.

73. a. The client's natural haircolor will determine the undertones that are still present and that will affect how the hair receives the pigment.

74. a. Orange is best neutralized by blue, its complement on the color wheel.

75. d. Only oxidative hair color can lighten and apply color in a single step.

76. a. After lightening, each hair strand becomes somewhat coarser (fatter) and more pliable.

77. a. Because the client's hair is still predominantly dark, it will be necessary to choose a color that is lighter than the desired level to achieve a natural-looking result.

78. a. The main purpose of record keeping is to ensure consistent results for the client.

79. a. If the rinse water or the relaxer gets into the client's eyes, rinse with water and refer the client to a doctor.

80. c. Clients who receive regular facial treatments can expect them to help increase circulation, activate glandular activity, relax the nerves, maintain muscle tone, and strengthen weak muscle tissues.

81. b. Part the hair first from the forehead to the nape of the neck.

82. d. If you thin the hair near the hairline, the thinning will show.

83. b. The head form or the shape of the head or skull, also referred to as the head shape, plays a major role in guiding you to the desired end result.

84. d. Top and crown layering of long hair prevents the hair from lying too flat on the head, making the look fuller.

85. b. Finger waving is a wet setting technique and no permanent texture change is initiated through a chemical reaction.

86. a. A shadow wave is a shallow wave with low ridges.

87. a. Acid waves process with heat.

88. d. Exothermic waves create an exothermic chemical reaction, with the addition of an activator that heats up the perming solution and speeds up the processing.

89. a. The smaller the roller, the tighter the resulting curl.

90. d. The client with a prominent nose needs softness around her face.

91. b. The aim should be to add as much width as possible.

92. c. Before making a thermal wave, comb the hair in the direction of the wave.

93. c. To form a half-base curl, begin by holding the hair at an angle of 90 degrees from the scalp.

94. b. Using vaporizing irons on hair that has been pressed will make it very curly again.

95. b. Use a vent brush to create a lift effect at the crown.

96. d. The heat of a pressing comb keeps it sterile as long as it is kept free of dirt and debris.

97. b. The hair can burn or smoke if it is pressed when wet.

98. a. The correct procedure is to begin at the front hair line, extend the tape measure to a point just above one ear, and continue down to the lower back of the head, above the other ear, and back to the starting point.

99. d. In the maturation stage the lock is totally closed at the end and the hair is tightly meshed and after several years of maturation, the lock may start to weaken or come apart at the ends.

100. a. A chignon is a knot or coil of synthetic hair, usually worn with another hairpiece.

8 ▶ Cosmetology Advancement Foundation's National Industry Skill Standards

CHAPTER SUMMARY

In this chapter, you will find the Cosmetology Advancement Foundation's (CAF) National Industry Skill Standards for entry-level cosmetologists, along with some information about the foundation itself.

THE FOLLOWING NATIONAL Industry Skill Standards are printed with the permission of the Cosmetology Advancement Foundation. For the past several years, the CAF has been working hard to include these standards in textbooks and other educational cosmetology materials, with the goal of state boards universally accepting the standards and including them in curriculum, therefore promoting more uniform requirements for licensed cosmetologists around the United States.

The mission statement of the Cosmetology Advancement Foundation is:

"The Cosmetology Advancement Foundation was created to support industry unity and initiatives that contribute to positive image and advance of cosmetology."

CAF continues to reach out to the community at large, promoting a positive image for cosmetologists and bringing greater awareness about the profession to schools and colleges around the country.

National Industry Skill Standards

Cosmetology Industry

Skill Standards and Illustrative Task Statements

Skill	Level of Standard	Illustrative Task Statement
Reading Comprehension *Understanding written sentences and paragraphs in work related documents*	3	(1) Read and complete forms for employment, financial records, licenses, etc. (3) Read manufacturer directions, procedures, and precautions of selected products to perform a cosmetology service
Active Listening *Listening to what other people are saying and asking questions as appropriate*	6	(1) Communicate with vendors and manufacturers to obtain product information (2) Communicate with co-workers to encourage a team atmosphere and team efforts (3) Schedule client appointments (4) Observe and listen to client to determine cosmetology needs (6) Utilize client feedback as a self-evaluation of performance
Writing *Communicating effectively with others in writing as indicated by the needs of the audience*	2	(1) Maintain a waiting list for client appointments (1) Maintain client records in written form (2) Fill out forms such as applications (2) Write professional letters to clients

Skill	Level of Standard	Illustrative Task Statement
Speaking *Talking to others to effectively convey information*	4	(1) Greet clients and give an overview of services and products available (2) Discuss maintenance and care of hair after services; including products, restrictions, and special care (4) Consult with clients to determine their cosmetology needs
Mathematics *Using mathematics to solve problems*	3	(1) Complete sales ticket for services and/or products (2) Maintain records of income, including tips, and expenses (2) Price products for resale (3) Determine most economical sale of products, using division and conversion units. (3) Determine formula of solution for hair texture, porosity, and elasticity (3) Use geometry techniques to determine proper hair cut techniques
Critical Thinking *Using logic and analysis to identify the strengths and weaknesses of different approaches*	4	(1) Establish time requirements and prices for services (2) Maintain an appointment schedule (3) Evaluate client and their requests to determine appropriate services and/or products (4) Determine reactions to solutions, procedures, or products by observing the client (4) Self-evaluation of performance and determining new approaches for improvement
Active Learning *Working with new material or information to grasp its implications*	4	(1) Subscribe to professional cosmetology journals and attend seminars to learn new hair designs and techniques (2) Learn about products through personal use (3) Use client feedback as a self-evaluation of performance (4) Consult with client to determine needs and expectations for services
Learning Strategies *Using multiple approaches when learning or teaching new things*	1	(1) Use a variety of teaching strategies to show clients how to care for hair, skin, and/or nails

Skill	Level of Standard	Illustrative Task Statement
Monitoring *Assessing how well one is doing when learning or doing something*	4	(1) Maintains and uses a reminder system for daily schedules and tasks (2) Monitor various procedures to assure positive results (3) Determine reactions to solutions, procedures, or products by observing client (4) Utilize client feedback as a self-evaluation of performance
Social Perceptiveness *Being aware of othersí reactions and understanding why they react the way they do*	4	(2) Demonstrates respect for individual differences (3) Assist co-workers in resolving problems or conflicts (4) By observing clients, determine reactions to solutions, procedures, or products
Coordination *Adjusting actions in relation to othersí actions*	3	(1) Maintain a work schedule and an appointment reminder system (2) Schedule client appointments (3) Adjust procedures to fit client needs and expectations
Persuasion *Persuading others to approach things differently*	2	(1) Suggest products and services or sell added services (2) Encourage client to change hairstyle, beauty regimen, or try a new service
Instructing *Teaching others how to do something*	1	(1) Teach client how to maintain hair care, nail care, or skin care and proper product usage
Service Orientation *Actively looking for ways to help people*	5	(1) Greet clients and offer them refreshments (2) Accommodate waiting customers (3) Consult with clients to determine needs and expectations (4) Discuss available alternatives with the client, when their expectations cannot be met (5) Provide services to meet the needs and expectations of clients
Problem Identification *Identifying the nature of problems*	4	(1) Review manufacturer procedures, directions, and precautions before performing service (2) Determine reactions to solutions, procedures, or products by observing client (3) Assist co-workers in resolving problems or conflicts (4) Identify signs of adverse health/safety conditions and take appropriate action or precautions (4) Analyze client needs for products and/or services

Information Gathering *Knowing how to find information and identifying essential information*	3	(1) Locate information sources for current cosmetology trends and information (2) Ask co-workers and other professionals for information and assistance (3) Consult manufacturer's directions and safety precautions for products
Information Organization *Finding ways to structure or classify multiple pieces of information*	2	(1) Organize work area based on sequence of services, use of equipment, or other logical approach (2) Organize client information to assure efficient access to critical personal and health information (2) Utilize system for important information such as client records, income, tips, and expense records, etc.
Idea Generation *Generating a number of different approaches to problems*	3	(1) Describe different hairstyles to achieve a client's desired look (3) Incorporate various marketing strategies into a client development plan
Idea Evaluation *Evaluating the likely success of an idea in relation to the demands of the situation*	2	(1) Select products according to hair and scalp type and condition (2) Recommend services and products based on client's needs and expectations
Solution Appraisal *Observing and evaluating the outcomes of a problem solution to identify lessons learned or redirect efforts*	2	(1) Determine problems and outcomes by communicating with clients (2) Observe clients to determine reactions to solutions, procedures, or products (2) Gives and receives feedback to increase cooperation
Operations Analysis *Analyzing needs and product requirements to create a design*	2	(1) Determine hair design through listening to client's requests (2) Recommend products and/or services to meet the client's needs and expectations (2) Use business records to evaluate business growth
Operation and Control *Controlling operations of equipment or systems*	2	(2) Use a variety of instruments and equipment to achieve various services
Equipment Maintenance *Performing routine maintenance and determining when and what kind of maintenance is needed*	1	(1) Change blades for razors (1) Sanitize instruments and equipment (1) Oil clippers/scissors
Visioning *Developing an image of how a system should work under ideal conditions*	3	(1) Understand how to conduct business using a salon team approach (2) Implement a time management plan based on normal working situations (3) Develop image of finished style needed to meet client's expectations

Skill	Level of Standard	Illustrative Task Statement
Identification of Key Causes *Identifying the things that must be changed to achieve a goal*	4	(1) Provide and encourage the use of a suggestion box (2) Contact past clients to determine customer satisfaction (3) Review processes and procedures while providing client services (4) Analyze records of performance and client retention to determine areas of improvement
Judgement and Decision Making *Weighing the relative costs and benefits of a potential action*	4	(1) Maintain professionalism while interacting with clients and co-workers (2) Identify precautions and safety measures needed to protect the client (2) Maintain an appointment schedule (3) Make decisions and plan actions based on the well-being of the entire salon or team (4) Develop a marketing, client development, or business plan
Time Management *Managing one's own time and/or time of others*	4	(1) Define time allotments for various services (2) Develop and maintain an appointment schedule (3) Adjust services or actions to accommodate adverse time conditions (3) Use available time to benefit salon operations or professional development, when client's fail to show or cancel appointments (4) Evaluate appointment records and past performance to determine one's time efficiency
Management of Financial Resources *Determining how money will be spent to get the work done, and accounting for these expenditures*	3	(1) Determine potential income and expenses based on income structures (commission vs. salaries), service times, product usage, and other variables (2) Maintain financial records, such as daily cash report, weekly sales, monthly statements, and tax reports (3) Manage income to successfully meet expenses and provisions for future endeavors
Management of Material Resources *Obtaining and seeing to the appropriate use of equipment, facilities, and materials needed to do certain work*	2	(1) Properly use salon equipment, facilities, and products (2) Maintain product supply for client services, purchasing products in bulk quantities when appropriate (2) Inventory retail product supply and places orders accordingly
Hair Care *Performing routine care to enhance condition and appearance of hair*	3	(1) Shampoo and condition hair (2) Determine hair condition and type based on observation (3) Recommend or provide solutions to improper hair care regimens

Skill	Level of Standard	Illustrative Task Statement
Skin Care *Performing routine care to enhance condition and appearance of skin*	3	(1) Cleanse skin (1) Operate simple facial equipment (2) Determine skin condition and type based on observation (3) Apply basic skin treatment for the improvement of skin, including cleansing, toning, moisturizing, and massage
Nail Care *Performing routine care to enhance condition and appearance of nails*	3	(1) Give hand massage and cleanse nails (2) Manipulate the cuticle (3) Shape, condition, and polish nails
Hair Designing *Arrange hair to achieve artistic design*	4	(1) Blow dry hair (2) Use wet & dry setting techniques to achieve final hair design. Use thermal tools and products to achieve final hair design (3) Arrange hair through various styling techniques to achieve final hair design (4) Design hair dependent on the client's facial shape, individual style, and expectations
Hair Cutting *Shorten or shape hair using a variety of hair cutting techniques and equipment*	4	(1) Cut a one-length hair style (2) Cut hair utilizing angles and sectioning; layered, graduated hair styles (4) Create length and shape dependent on hair texture, condition, growth pattern, and facial shape
Hair Removal *Removing hair using various techniques*	3	(1) Prep skin for hair removal and remove hair from the body. Perform aftercare (2) Wax and tweeze hair to shape the eyebrow (3) Use depilatory products to remove hair from the body
Hair Additions *Adding hair using various techniques*	3	(1) Fit and style a hair piece (2) Select an appropriate hair piece based on client needs and characteristics (3) Use hair addition techniques to enhance hair volume
Chemical Reconstruction *Altering hair structure using chemical processes*	3	(2) Choose products and services for hair reconstruction dependent on the client's needs (3) Apply products and techniques to produce or remove wave and curl formation
Hair Coloring *Altering hair color using a variety of processes*	3	(1) Interpret color charts to determine appropriate formula needs (2) Analyze hair condition and recognize evidence of previous hair treatments (3) Apply color products to hair

▶ Performance Guidelines

Five critical job functions were identified for the entry-level cosmetologist. Twenty performance guidelines were developed for these job functions. Each guideline includes performance indicators, the representative skill standards, knowledge, and abilities. Peformance indicators are observable task statements that are indicative of successful performance of the guideline and job function. The following are the performance guidelines divided by critical job function.

CLIENT SERVICE *The entry-level cosmetologist provides a variety of services to meet the needs, well being, and satisfaction of clients.*

The entry level cosmetologist must consult with clients to determine their needs and preferences as it relates to cosmetology services.

Performance Indicators:

Greets client and give an overview of services and products available

Observes and asks questions to determine the client's needs and expectations

Discusses the benefits and/or features of products and services

Uses visual media as appropriate to enhance communication

After establishing services to be performed and prices, ask for the client's permission to proceed

General Work Skills:

	Industry Standard:
Active listening	6
Speaking	4
Social perceptiveness	4
Service orientation	5
Problem identification	4
Information gathering	3
Idea generation	4
Judgment and decision making	4
Industry-Specific Skills:	
Hair care	3
Nail care	3
Skin care	3

Generalized Work Activities:

Getting Information needed to do the job

Performing for or working directly with the public

Work Styles:

Achievement
Energy
Cooperation
Concern for others
Social orientation
Self-control
Independence
Analytical thinking

Knowledge:

Customer and personal service
Communication and media

Industry-Specific Knowledge:
Anatomy and Physiology

Abilities:

Oral comprehension
Oral expression
Originality
Problem sensitivity
Deductive reasoning
Auditory attention -
Speech recognition
Speech clarity

CLIENT SERVICE *The entry level cosmetologist provides a variety of services to meet the needs, well-being, and satisfaction of clients.*

The entry level cosmetologist must conduct services in a safe environment and take measures to prevent the spread of infectious and contagious disease.

General Work Skill:

	Industry Standard:
Active listening	6
Social perceptiveness	4
Service orientation	5
Problem identification	4
Judgement and decision making	4

Knowledge:
Customer and personal service
Public safety and security

Abilities:
Oral comprehension
Problem sensitivity
Deductive reasoning
Selective attention

Performance Indicators:
Work area is clean and organized before each service
Safety and sanitary precautions are taken to protect clients and self
Personal protective measures, such as gloves, smock, etc. are used
Special steps to ensure client safety are taken when necessary
Client is draped and properly prepared for service
Equipment and instruments are sterilized and maintained prior to each use
Signs of infectious or contagious disease are identified and appropriate action or precautions are taken

Generalized Work Activities:
Make decisions and solving problems
Organizing, planning, and prioritizing work
Assisting and caring for others
Performing for or working directly with the public

Work Styles:
Initiative
Concern for others
Dependability
Attention to detail
Integrity
Analytical thinking

CLIENT SERVICE *The entry-level cosmetologist provides a variety of services to meet the needs, well being, and satisfaction of clients.*

The entry-level cosmetologist must interact effectively with co-workers as part of a team.

Performance Indicators:
Effectively works with co-workers to resolve conflicts
Gives and receives feedback to enhance cooperation
Shows respect for personal differences in others
Takes initiative to facilitate cooperation and compromise within the group
Involves and motivates co-workers in group efforts
Participates in team activities, to advance team goals
Make decisions and plan actions based on the well-being of the entire salon or team

General Work Skill:

	Industry Standard:
Active listening	6
Speaking	4
Social perceptiveness	4
Coordination	3
Service orientation	5
Problem identification	4
Information gathering	3
Solution appraisal	2
Judgment and decision making	4

Knowledge:
Administration and Management
Customer and Personal Service
Psychology

Abilities:
Oral comprehension
Written comprehension
Oral expression
Written expression
Problem sensitivity
Auditory attention
Speech recognition
Speech clarity

Work Styles:
Cooperation
Concern for others
Social orientation
Self-control
Adaptability/flexibility
Dependability
Integrity
Independence

Generalized Work Activities:
Getting information needed to do the job
Communicating with supervisors, peers, or subordinates
Establishing and maintaining interpersonal relationships
Resolving conflicts and negotiating with others

CLIENT SERVICE: *The entry-level cosmetologist provides a variety of services to meet the needs, well being, and satisfaction of clients.*

The entry level cosmetologist must effectively manage their time to provide efficient client service.

Performance Indicators:

Develops and uses accurate time allotments when scheduling client services

Demonstrates a respect for client's time by minimizing waiting time and performing services in appropriate time

Maintains a waiting list to fill changes in schedule

Maintains and uses a reminder system for daily schedules and tasks

Uses available time to benefit salon operations or professional development, when client's fail to show or cancel appointments

Generalized Work Activities:

Getting information needed to do the job

Monitoring processes, materials, or surroundings

Judging the qualities of objects, services, or persons

Making decisions and solving problems

Thinking creatively

Developing objectives and strategies

Organizing, planning, and prioritizing work

Communicating with supervisors, peers, or subordinates

Communicating with persons outside the organization

General Work Skills:

	Industry Standard:
Active listening	6
Critical thinking	4
Monitoring	4
Social perceptiveness	4
Coordination	3
Service orientation	5
Judgment and decision making	4
Time Management	4

Work Styles:

Persistence

Initiative

Energy

Leadership orientation

Cooperation

Concern for others

Social orientation

Adaptability/flexibility

Dependability

Attention to detail

Independence

Analytical thinking

Knowledge:

Administration and Management

Customer and Personal Service

Abilities:

Oral comprehension

Written comprehension

Written expression

Problem sensitivity

Deductive reasoning

Memorization

Selective attention

Time sharing

CLIENT SERVICE *The entry-level cosmetologist provides a variety of services to meet the needs, well being, and satisfaction of clients.*

The entry level cosmetologist must take necessary steps to develop and retain clients.

Performance Indicators:
Develops a plan or strategy to retain clients and encourage the return of customers
Actively seeks client feedback and uses it as self-evaluation of performance
Develops a client record system and maintains current information on clients
Contacts past clients to determine customer satisfaction

General Work Skills:

	Industry Standard:
Active listening	6
Writing	2
Critical thinking	4
Monitoring	4
Service orientation	5
Identification of key causes	4
Judgment and decision making	4

Knowledge:
Sales and marketing
Customer and personal service

Abilities:
Oral comprehension
Oral expression
Written expression
Problem sensitivity

Generalized Work Activities:
Judging the qualities of objects, services, or persons
Analyzing data and information
Developing objectives and strategies
Documenting/Recording information
Communication with persons outside the organization
Establishing and maintaining interpersonal relationships
Selling or influencing others
Performing for or working directly with the public

Work Styles:
Achievement/effort
Persistence
Initiative
Energy
Leadership
Orientation
Social orientation
Dependability
Independence

BUSINESS OPERATIONS *The entry-level cosmetologist participates in business operations including marketing, business development, and maintaining records.*

The entry level cosmetologist must effectively market professional salon products.

Performance Indicators:
Identify potential needs of clients and recommend appropriate products
Discusses products and their benefits with clients
Offers clients "best buy" suggestions based on cost per unit
Arrange products and merchandise to promote retail sales
Promotes the use of products through personal use
Maintains current information on products and manufacturers

General Work Skills:

	Industry Standard:
Reading comprehension	3
Active listening	6
Speaking	4
Mathematics	3
Critical thinking	4
Active learning	4
Problem identification	4
Information gathering	3
Information organization	2
Operations analysis	2
Judgment and decision making	4
Management of material resources	2

Generalized Work Activities:
Judging the qualities of objects, services, or persons
Evaluating information for compliance to standards
Processing information
Making decisions and solving problems
Updating and using job-relevant knowledge
Handling and moving objects
Communicating with persons outside the organization
Performing administrative activities
Monitoring and controlling resources

Work Styles:
Achievement/effort
Persistence
Initiative
Adaptability/flexibility
Dependability
Attention to detail
Independence
Innovation
Analytical thinking

Knowledge:
Administration and management
Sales and marketing

Abilities:
Oral comprehension
Written comprehension
Oral expression
Written expression
Deductive reasoning
Inductive reasoning
Information ordering
Mathematical reasoning
Number facility

BUSINESS OPERATIONS *The entry-level cosmetologist participates in business operations including marketing, business development, and maintaining records.*

The entry level cosmetologist must maintain business records on client development, income, and expenses.

Performance Indicators:

Utilize a system for maintaining records of income, tips, and expenses

Use records to determine business growth

Accurately completes tax forms and reporting requirements

Maintain an organized system of important documents

General Work Skills:

	Industry Standard:
Reading comprehension	3
Writing	2
Mathematics	3
Critical thinking	4
Monitoring	6
Information organization	2
Operations analysis	2
Judgment and decision making	4
Management of financial resources	3

Knowledge:

Administration and management

Clerical

Economics and accounting

Abilities:

Written comprehension

Written expression

Problem sensitivity

Deductive reasoning

Information ordering

Number facility

General Work Activities:

Getting information needed to do the job

Evaluating information for compliance to standards

Processing information

Analyzing data or information

Making decisions and solving problems

Interacting with computers

Documenting/Recording information

Performing administrative activities

Monitoring and controlling resources

Work Styles:

Achievement/effort

Initiative

Dependability

Attention to detail

Integrity

Independence

Analytical thinking

PRODUCT KNOWLEDGE, USE, AND SAFETY *The entry-level cosmetologist must demonstrate safe and effective use of a variety of cosmetology products.*

The entry level cosmetologist must safely use a variety of salon products while providing client services.

Performance Indicators:
Uses appropriate protective measures to protect self and client against product hazards

Discusses benefits and features of products with clients.

Selects products according to the client's hair and scalp condition

Conducts clean-up procedures including proper storage and disposal of products according to environmental and health safety guidelines

Generalized Work Activities:
Getting information needed to do the job

Identifying objects, materials, or surroundings

Monitoring processes, materials, or surroundings

Inspecting equipment, structures, or materials

Estimating the characteristics of materials, products, events, or information

Judging the qualities of objects, services, or persons

Evaluating information for compliance to standards

Processing information

Making decisions and solving problems

Implementing ideas, programs, systems, or products

Interpreting the meaning of information for others

Work Styles:
Cooperation

Concern for others

Social orientation

Self-control

Adaptability/flexibility

Dependability

Integrity

Independence

General Work Skills:

	Industry Standard:
Reading comprehension	3
Critical thinking	4
Active learning	4
Problem identification	4
Information gathering	3
Solution appraisal	3
Operations analysis	2
Testing	3
Judgment and decision making	4
Management of material resources	2

Industry-specific Skills

Hair care	3
Skin care	3
Nail care	3
Chemical hair reconstruction	3
Hair coloring	3
Hair removal	3

Knowledge:
Chemistry

Biology

Public safety and security

Industry Specific Knowledge:
Product Knowledge

Safety/Health Regulations

Abilities:
Oral comprehension

Written comprehension

Oral expression

Written expression

Problem sensitivity

Deductive reasoning

Information ordering

Memorization

PRODUCT KNOWLEDGE, USE, AND SAFETY *The entry-level cosmetologist must demonstrate safe and effective use of a variety of cosmetology products.*

The entry level cosmetologist must efficiently manage product supply for salon use and retail sales.

Performance Indicators:

Maintain adequate product supply for client services

Avoids product waste by using appropriate amount of product

Purchases products in bulk quantities for salon use, when appropriate

Routinely inventories retail product supply and places orders accordingly

General Work Skills:

	Industry Standard:
Reading comprehension	3
Mathematics	3
Critical thinking	4
Monitoring	6
Problem identification	4
Information gathering	3
Information organization	2
Operations analysis	2
Judgment and decision making	4
Management of material resources	2

Knowledge:

Administration and management

Sales and marketing

Industry-Specific Knowledge:

Product knowledge

Abilities:

Written comprehension

Deductive reasoning

Inductive reasoning

Information ordering

Mathematical reasoning

Number facility

Work Styles:

Achievement/effort

Persistence

Initiative

Adaptability/flexibility

Dependability

Attention to detail

Independence

Innovation

Analytical thinking

Generalized Work Activities:

Judging the qualities of objects, services, or persons

Evaluating information for compliance to standards

Processing information

Making decisions and solving problems

Updating and using job-relevant knowledge

Handling and moving objects

Communicating with persons outside the organization

Performing administrative activities

Monitoring and controlling resources

FASHION, ART, AND TECHNICAL DESIGN *The entry-level cosmetologist produces fashion, art, and technical design by providing a variety of cosmetology services.*

The entry level cosmetologist must provide basic skin care services.

Performance Indicators:

Cleanses skin using appropriate products and proper technique

Applies toners and moisturizers appropriate to skin type and condition

Use proper technique in facial massage therapy

Discuss with client proper skin care

General Work Skills:

	Industry Standard:
Critical thinking	4
Monitoring	6
Social perceptiveness	4
Service orientation	5
Judgment and decision making	4

Industry-Specific Skills:

Skin Care

Generalized Work Activities:

Monitoring process, materials, or surroundings

Performing general physical activities

Communicating with persons outside the organization

Establishing and maintaining interpersonal relationships

Assisting and caring for others

Performing for or working directly with the public

Providing consultation and advice to others

Work Styles:

Initiative

Energy

Leadership orientation

Cooperation

Concern for others

Social orientation

Attention to detail

Independence

Analytical thinking

Knowledge:

Customer and personal service

Chemistry

Industry-Specific Knowledge:

Product knowledge

Anatomy and Physiology

Facials

Sterilization, Sanitation, & Bacteriology

Abilities:

Oral comprehension

Oral expression

Problem sensitivity

Finger dexterity

FASHION, ART, AND TECHNICAL DESIGN *The entry-level cosmetologist produces fashion, art, and technical design by providing a variety of cosmetology services.*

The entry level cosmetologist must provide basic manicure and pedicure.

Performance Indicators:
Sanitize area, self, and client's hands
Sanitize implements (instruments) before each use
Shape, condition, and polish nails to the satisfaction of client
Massage and moisturize hands, wrists, and arms
Discuss with client proper nail care

General Work Skills:	Industry Standard:
Active listening	6
Speaking	4
Monitoring	6
Social perceptiveness	4
Service orientation	5
Judgment and decision making	4

Industry-Specific Skills:
Nail Care

Generalized Work Activities:
Communicating with persons outside the organization
Establishing and maintaining interpersonal relationships
Assisting and caring for others
Performing for or working directly with the public

Work Styles:
Initiative
Energy
Leadership orientation
Cooperation
Concern for others
Social orientation
Attention to detail
Independence
Analytical thinking

Knowledge:
Customer and personal service
Public safety and security
Industry-Specific Knowledge:
Product knowledge
Anatomy and Physiology
Manicures
Sterilization, Sanitation, & Bacteriology

Abilities:
Problem sensitivity
Arm-hand steadiness
Finger dexterity
Near vision

FASHION, ART, AND TECHNICAL DESIGN *The entry-level cosmetologist produces fashion, art, and technical design by providing a variety of cosmetology services.*

The entry level cosmetologist must apply appropriate cosmetics to enhance a client's appearance.

Performance Indicators:

Sanitize implements and prepare products before each service

Properly prepare skin before make-up application

Apply foundation and color according to client's individual skin condition, color palate, and style

Discuss with client proper makeup techniques

General Work Skills:

	Industry Standard:
Speaking	4
Critical thinking	4
Monitoring	4
Social perceptiveness	4
Instructing	1
Service orientation	5
Visioning	3
Judgment and decision making	4

Industry-Specific Skills:

Skin care

Generalized Work Activities:

Getting information needed to do the job

Monitoring processes, materials, or surroundings

Making decisions and solving problems

Thinking creatively

Communicating with persons outside the organizations

Establishing and maintaining interpersonal relationships

Performing for or working directly with the public

Work Styles:

Initiative

Energy

Leadership orientation

Cooperation

Concern for others

Social orientation

Adaptability/flexibility

Attention to detail

Independence

Innovation

Analytical thinking

Knowledge:

Customer and personal service

Design

Fine arts

Public safety and security

Industry-Specific Knowledge:

Product knowledge

Makeup Design

Abilities:

Fluency of ideas

Originality

Problem sensitivity

Visualization

Arm-hand steadiness

Visual color discrimination

FASHION, ART, AND TECHNICAL DESIGN *The entry-level cosmetologist produces fashion, art, and technical design by providing a variety of cosmetology services.*

The entry level cosmetologist must provide a haircut in accordance with a client's needs or expectations.

Performance Indicators:
Conceive vision of finished style and appropriate steps to accomplish it
Select and prepare equipment and products prior to beginning service
Applies a variety of cutting techniques to achieve the client's desired haircut
Accomplishes service in a standard amount of time
Maintains attention to detail throughout haircutting process

General Work Skills:

	Industry Standard:
Coordination	3
Operation analysis	2
Equipment selection	3
Operation and control	2
Visioning	3
Judgment and decision making	4

Industry-Specific Skills:

Hair care	3
Hair cutting	3

Generalized Work Activities:
Getting information needed to do the job
Thinking creatively
Updating and using job-relevant knowledge
Performing general physical activities
Handling and moving objects
Controlling machines and processes
Implementing ideas, programs, systems, or products
Interpreting the meaning of information for others

Work Styles:
Achievement/effort
Persistence
Initiative
Energy
Cooperation
Concern for others
Social orientation
Self-control
Stress tolerance
Adaptability/flexibility
Dependability
Attention to detail
Independence
Innovation
Analytical thinking

Knowledge:
Design
Mechanical
Fine arts

Industry-Specific Knowledge:
Anatomy and Physiology
Hairstyling
Sterilization, Sanitation, & Bacteriology
Health/Safety Regulations

Abilities:
Problem sensitivity
Deductive reasoning
Selective attention

FASHION, ART, AND TECHNICAL DESIGN *The entry-level cosmetologist produces fashion, art, and technical design by providing a variety of cosmetology services.*

The entry level cosmetologist must provide styling and finishing techniques to complete a hairstyle to the satisfaction of the client.

Performance Indicators:
Conceive vision of desired look and appropriate techniques needed to achieve it
Use a variety of finishing techniques to achieve the client's desired hairstyle
Select appropriate equipment and products prior to beginning service
Instruct clients on procedures and/or products to insure their satisfaction and ability to recreate the style
Accomplishes service in a standard amount of time

General Work Skills:
	Industry Standard:
Critical thinking	4
Coordination	3
Problem identification	4
Idea generation	4
Operations analysis	2
Equipment selection	3
Visioning	3
Judgment and decision making	4

Industry Specific Skills:
Hair care	3
Hair designing	3

Generalized Work Activities:
Identifying objects, actions, and events
Estimating the characteristics of materials, products, events, or information
Making decisions and solving problems
Thinking creatively
Updating and using job-relevant knowledge
Performing general physical activities
Handling and moving objects
Controlling machines and processes
Implementing ideas, programs, systems, or products
Interpreting the meaning of information for others

Work Styles:
Achievement/effort
Persistence
Initiative
Social orientation
Self-control
Adaptability/flexibility
Dependability
Attention to detail
Independence
Innovation
Analytical thinking

Knowledge:
Design
Chemistry
Fine arts

Industry Specific Knowledge:
Product knowledge
Anatomy and Physiology
Hairstyling

Abilities:
Originality
Inductive reasoning
Visualization
Selective attention
Manual dexterity
Depth perception

FASHION, ART, AND TECHNICAL DESIGN *The entry-level cosmetologist produces fashion, art, and technical design by providing a variety of cosmetology services.*

The entry level cosmetologist must conduct a color service in accordance with a client's needs or expectations.

Performance Indicators:

Proper protective measures for both self and client are used for every service – i.e. gloves, smock, etc.

Equipment and products are selected and prepared before beginning service

Correct formula of solution is chosen according to hair texture, porosity, and elasticity

Manufacturer procedures, directions, and precautions are reviewed before performing service

Client is observed to determine adverse reactions to solutions, procedures, or products

Client is instructed on procedures and/or products to insure their continued satisfaction

Procedure is documented for client record, including colors and products used

	Industry Standard:
General Work Skills:	
Reading comprehension	3
Critical thinking	4
Coordination	3
Problem identification	4
Information gathering	3
Idea generation	4
Operations analysis	2
Equipment selection	3
Testing	3
Visioning	3
Judgment and decision making	4
Industry-Specific Skills;	
Hair care	3
Hair coloring	3

Generalized Work Activities:

Getting information needed to do the job

Identifying objects, actions, and events

Monitoring processes, materials, or surroundings

Estimating the characteristics of materials, products, events, or information

Making decisions and solving problems

Thinking creatively

Updating and using job-relevant knowledge

Performing general physical activities

Handling and moving objects

Controlling machines and processes

Implementing ideas, programs, systems, or products

Interpreting the meaning of information for others

Work Styles:

Achievement/effort

Persistence

Initiative

Social orientation

Self-control

Adaptability/flexibility

Dependability

Attention to detail

Independence

Innovation

Analytical thinking

Knowledge:

Design

Chemistry

Fine arts

Industry-Specific Knowledge:

Product knowledge

Anatomy and Physiology

Hair Coloring

Abilities:

Originality

Problem sensitivity

Inductive reasoning

Visualization

Selective attention

Manual dexterity

Finger dexterity

Near vision

Depth perception

FASHION, ART, AND TECHNICAL DESIGN *The entry-level cosmetologist produces fashion, art, and technical design by providing a variety of cosmetology services.*

The entry level cosmetologist must perform hair relaxation and wave formation techniques in accordance with the manufacturer directions.

Performance Indicator:

Proper protective measures for both self and client are used for every service—i.e., gloves, smock, etc.

Equipment and products are selected and prepared before beginning service

Correct technique or formula of solution is chosen according to hair texture, porosity, and elasticity

Manufacturer procedures, directions, and precautions are reviewed before performing service

A test of formula is correctly made with client's hair

Client is observed to determine adverse reactions to solutions, procedures, or products

Client is instructed on procedures and/or products to insure their continued satisfaction

Procedure is documented for client record, including colors and products used

Generalized Work Activities:

Getting information needed to do the job

Identifying objects, actions, and events

Monitoring processes, materials, or surroundings

Estimating the characteristics of materials, products, events, or information

Making decisions and solving problems

Thinking creative!

Updating and using job-relevant knowledge

Performing general physical activities

Handling and moving objects

Controlling machines and processes

Implementing ideas, programs, systems, or products

Interpreting the meaning of information for others.

General Work Skills:

	Industry Standard:
Reading comprehension	3
Critical thinking	4
Coordination	3
Problem identification	4
Information gathering	3
Idea generation	4
Operations analysis	2
Equipment selection	3
Testing	3
Visioning	3
Judgment and decision making	4

Industry Specific Skills:

Hair care	3
Chemical hair reconstruction	3
Hair designing	3

Work Styles:

Achievement/effort

Persistence

Initiative

Social orientation

Self-control

Adaptability/flexibility

Dependability

Attention to detail

Independence

Innovation

Analytical thinking

Knowledge:

Design

Chemistry

Fine arts

Industry-Specific Knowledge:

Anatomy and Physiology

Product knowledge

Hair Waving

Abilities:

Originality

Problem sensitivity

Inductive reasoning

Visualization

Selective attention

Manual dexterity

Finger dexterity

Near vision

FASHION, ART, AND TECHNICAL DESIGN *The entry-level cosmetologist produces fashion, art, and technical design by providing a variety of cosmetology services.*

The entry level cosmetologist must provide non-surgical hair additions.

Performance Indicators:

Select appropriate hairpiece according to client's individual needs and style

Properly fit, style, and adapt hairpiece to maintain a natural appearance

Instruct client on proper maintenance, application and removal of hairpiece

Use hair addition techniques to enhance hair volume

General Work Skills:	Industry Standard:
Critical thinking	4
Monitoring	6
Social perceptiveness	4
Coordination	3
Persuasion	2
Instructing	1
Service orientation	5
Solution appraisal	3
Visioning	3
Judgment and decision making	4
Industry-Specific Skills:	
Hair additions	3

Generalized Work Activities:

Monitoring processes, materials, or surroundings

Making decisions and solving problems

Thinking creatively

Communicating with persons outside the organization

Establishing and maintaining interpersonal relationships

Assisting and caring for others

Performing for or working directly with the public

Providing consultation and advice to others

Work Styles:

Initiative

Energy

Leadership orientation

Cooperation

Concern for others

Social orientation

Analytical thinking

Knowledge:

Customer and personal service

Industry-Specific Knowledge:

Hair replacement technology

Wiggery

Abilities:

Oral comprehension

Oral expression

Originality

Problem sensitivity

Visualization

Manual dexterity

Near Vision

FASHION, ART, AND TECHNICAL DESIGN *The entry-level cosmetologist produces fashion, art, and technical design by providing a variety of cosmetology services.*

The entry level cosmetologist must perform hair removal services.

General Work Skills:

	Industry Standard:
Active listening	6
Speaking	4
Critical thinking	4
Monitoring	6
Social perceptiveness	4
Service orientation	5
Problem identification	4
Operations analysis	2
Judgment and decision making	4

Industry-Specific Skills:

Skin care	3
Hair removal	3

Performance Indicators:

Select, sanitize, and prepare implements and products before beginning service

Perform skin analysis and properly prepare skin

Perform hair removal service to the satisfaction of client

Perform after care, such as moisturizer, anti-bacterial lotion, etc. to promote the comfort and satisfaction of the client

Knowledge:

Customer and personal service

Industry-Specific Knowledge:

Anatomy and Physiology

Sterilization, Sanitation, &

Electrology

Abilities:

Oral comprehension

Oral expression

Originality

Problem sensitivity

Visualization

Manual dexterity

Near Vision

Work Styles:

Initiative

Energy

Leadership orientation

Cooperation

Concern for others

Social orientation

Analytical thinking

Generalized Work Activities:

Monitoring processes, materials, or surroundings

Making decisions and solving problems

Communicating with persons outside the organization

Establishing and maintaining interpersonal relationships

Assisting and caring for others

Performing for or working directly with the public

Providing consultation and advice to others

PERSONAL DEVELOPMENT *The entry-level cosmetologist must continue to develop personally and professionally to maintain a competitive edge in the cosmetology industry.*

The entry level cosmetologist must participate in life-long learning to stay current of trends, technology, and techniques pertaining to the cosmetology industry.

Performance Indicators:
Routinely participates in industry related shows, fairs, seminars, etc.
Routinely participates in refresher courses for cosmetologists
Subscribes to cosmetology journals and professional organizations

Generalized Work Activities:
Getting information needed to do the job
Making decisions and solving problems
Thinking creatively
Updating and using job-relevant knowledge

Work Styles:
Achievement/effort
Persistence
Initiative
Leadership orientation
Cooperation
Concern for others
Social orientation
Adaptability/flexibility
Attention to detail
Independence
Innovation

General Work Skills:	Industry Standard:
Reading comprehension	3
Active listening	6
Critical thinking	4
Active learning	4
Social perceptiveness	3
Service orientation	5
Information gathering	3
Information organization	2
Idea generation	4
Idea evaluation	2
Visioning	3
Judgment and decision making	4

Abilities:
Oral comprehension
Written comprehension
Fluency of ideas
Originality
Information ordering
Visualization

Knowledge:
Customer and personal service
Design
Industry-Specific Knowledge:
Personal development

PERSONAL DEVELOPMENT *The entry-level cosmetologist must continue to develop personally and professionally to maintain a competitive edge in the cosmetology industry.*

The entry level cosmetologist must use appropriate methods to insure personal health and well-being

Performance Indicators:

Take appropriate measures to protect personal health —i.e., use of proper work attire

Adjust equipment and working area to meet individual requirements—i.e., adjust chair to proper height

Use equipment properly following appropriate ergonomics

General Work Skills:

	Industry Standard:
Critical thinking	4
Monitoring	6
Coordination	3
Problem identification	4
Information gathering	3
Operations analysis	2
Operation and control	2
Judgment and decision making	4

Generalized Work Activities:

Getting information needed to do the job

Monitoring processes, materials, or surroundings

Making decisions and solving problems

Performing general physical activities

Performing for or working directly with the public

Work Styles:

Achievement/effort

Initiative

Energy

Leadership orientation

Self-control

Attention to detail

Independence

Analytical thinking

Knowledge:

Public safety and security

Industry-Specific Knowledge:

Product knowledge

Industry-specific equipment knowledge

Abilities:

Deductive reasoning

Manual dexterity

CHAPTER

9 ▶ Licensing Requirements

SUMMARY

This chapter outlines cosmetology licensing requirements for all fifty states. It also lists state cosmetology agencies you can contact for more information about certification requirements.

THE FOLLOWING STATE-by-state table charts out the requirements for a license in Cosmetology. You will find contact information for your state's board of cosmetology, the licenses that state offers, the hours of training required, and the cost of getting licensed. Although all the information was correct at the time of publication, states do change requirements from time to time. Always confirm any information you find in this book with your state's board of cosmetology. See Chapter 1 for more information about the kinds of written exams your state offers.

STATE	CONTACT INFORMATION	AVAILABLE LICENSES	HOURS OF TRAINING REQUIRED	COST OF LICENSE
Alabama	Alabama Board of Cosmetology RSA Union Building 100 North Union Street #320 Montgomery, AL 36130 334-242-1918 fax: 334-242-1926 e-mail: cosmetology@aboc.state.al.us www.aboc.state.al.us	Cosmetologist Esthetician Nail technician Massage therapist	1,500 1,500 750 650	$80 $80 $80 $100

Alaska	State of Alaska Board of Barbers
	   and Hairdressers
	Department of Commerce and
	   Economic Development
	P.O. Box 110806
	Juneau, AK 99811
	907-465-2534
	fax: 907-465-2974
	e-mail: license@dced.state.ak.us
	www.dced.state.ak.us/occ/pbah.htm
		Esthetician
		Nail technician
		Hair dresser
			350
			250
			1,650
				$115
				$110
				N/A

Arizona	Arizona State Board of Cosmetology 1721 East Broadway Tempe, AZ 85282 602-784-4539 ext. 227 fax: 602-255-3680 www.azleg.state.az.us	Cosmetologist Esthetician Nail technician	1,600 600 600	$18 $15 $12
Arkansas	Arkansas State Board of Cosmetology 101 East Capital Avenue, #108 Little Rock, AR 72201 501-682-2168 fax: 501-682-5640 e-mail: cosmomail.state.ar.us www.state.ar.us	Cosmetologist Electrologist Esthetician Nail technician Massage therapist	1,500 600 600 600 500	$12 $12 $12 $12 $30–45
California	California State Bureau of Barbering and Cosmetology 400 R Street, Suite 5100 (95814) Sacramento, CA 94244-2260 916-445-0916 fax: 916-323-5037 www.dca.ca.gov/barber	Cosmetologist Electrologist Esthetician Nail technician	1,600 600 600 400	$40 $40 $40 $40

STATE	CONTACT INFORMATION	AVAILABLE LICENSES	HOURS OF TRAINING REQUIRED	COST OF LICENSE
Colorado	Colorado Office of Barber & Cosmetologist Licensing 1560 Broadway, #1340 Denver, CO 80202 303-894-7772 fax: 303-894-7802 www.state.co.us/gov_dir	Cosmetologist Esthetician Nail technician	1,450 550 350	$32 $32 $32
Connecticut	Connecticut Department of Public Health 410 Capital Avenue, MS #12 APP P.O. Box 340308 Hartford, CT 06134-0308 860-509-7569 fax: 860-509-8457 www.state.ct.us/otlg	Cosmetologist Nail technician Massage therapist	1,500 150 500	$25 $25 $100
Delaware	Delaware Board of Cosmetology Cannon Building 861 Silver Lake Boulevard, Suite 203 Dover, DE 19904 800-273-9500 or 302-739-4522, ext. 218 fax: 860-509-8457 or 302-739-2711 e-mail: gaylemelvin@state.de.us www.professionallicensing.state.de.us/boards/cosmetology/index.shtml	Cosmetologist Electrologist Esthetician Nail technician Massage therapist	1,500 600 300 125 500	$38 $28.80 $28.20 $28.80 $222
District of Columbia	District of Columbia Consumer & Regulatory Affairs Occupational & Professional Licensing 941 North Capitol Street NW, Suite 7200 Washington, DC 20002 202-442-4320 fax: 202-442-4528 www.dcra.org/main.shtm	Cosmetologist Esthetician Nail technician Massage therapist	1,500 350 350 500	$60 $305 $30 $95

STATE	CONTACT INFORMATION	AVAILABLE LICENSES	HOURS OF TRAINING REQUIRED	COST OF LICENSE
Florida	Florida Board of Cosmetology Department of Professional Regulation Northwood Centre 1940 North Monroe Street Tallahassee, FL 32399 850-488-5702 fax: 850-922-6959 e-mail: julie.baker@dbpr.state.fl.us www.state.fl.us/dbpr	Cosmetologist Esthetician Nail technician Massage therapist	1,200 260 240 500	$30 $35 $35 $100
	Board of Medicine, Electrolysis Council Department of Health 850-245-4373	Electrologist	320	$505
Georgia	Georgia State Board of Cosmetology 237 Coliseum Drive Macon, GA 31217-3858 478-207-1430 fax: 478-207-1442 www.sos.state.ga.us	Cosmetologist Nail technician Esthetician	1,500 (school) or 3,000 (apprentice) 525 (school) or 1,050 (apprentice) 1,000 (school) or 2,000 (apprentice)	$45 N/A N/A
Hawaii	Hawaii Professional Vocational Licensing Commerce & Consumer Affairs 1010 Richards Street P.O. Box 3469 Honolulu, HI 96801 808-586-3000 fax: 808-586-3031 www.state.hi.us/dcca	Cosmetologist Electrologist Esthetician Massage therapist Nail technician	1,800 (school) or 3,600 (apprentice) 600 (school) or 800 (apprentice) 600 (school) or 1,200 (apprentice) 570 350 (school) or 700 (apprentice)	$100 $120 $100 $120 $100

STATE	CONTACT INFORMATION	AVAILABLE LICENSES	HOURS OF TRAINING REQUIRED	COST OF LICENSE
Idaho	Idaho Department of Self-Governing Affairs Owyhee Plaza 1109 Main Street, Suite 220 Boise, ID 83702 208-334-3233 fax: 208-334-3945 www2.state.id.us/ibol/cos.htm	Cosmetologist Electrologist Esthetician Nail technician	2,000 800 600 300	$25 $27 $27 $25
Illinois	Illinois Department of Professional Regulations 320 West Washington Street, 3rd Floor Springfield, IL 62786 217-782-8556 fax: 217-557-8073 e-mail: tsanders@dpr084r1.state.il.us www.dpr.state.il.us	Cosmetologist Esthetician Nail technician	1,500 750 350	$45 $45 $45
Indiana	Indiana Professional Licensing Agency Government Center South 302 West Washington Street Room E 034 Indianapolis, IN 46204-2700 317-232-2980 fax: 317-232-5559 www.ai.org/pla/index.html	Cosmetologist Esthetician Nail technician Electrologist	1,500 700 300 300	$40 $40 $40 $40
Iowa	Iowa Department of Public Health Cosmetology Board of Iowa Lucas State Office Building Des Moines, IA 50319 515-281-4416 fax: 515-281-3121 e-mail: dsuchy@idph.state.ia.us www.state.ia.us/idph_pl/index.html	Cosmetologist Electrologist Esthetician Massage therapist Nail technician	2,100 425 600 500 325	$25 $25 $25 $100 $25

STATE	CONTACT INFORMATION	AVAILABLE LICENSES	HOURS OF TRAINING REQUIRED	COST OF LICENSE
Kansas	Kansas State Board of Cosmetology	Cosmetologist	1,500	$45
	714 Southwest Jackson, Suite 100	Electrologist	1,000 (apprentice)	$35
	Topeka, KS 66603-3714			
	785-296-3155	Esthetician	650	$30
	fax: 785-296-3002	Massage therapist	1,200 (apprentice)	$100
	e-mail: kboc@ink.org			
	www.ink.org/public/kboc/	Nail technician	350	$30
Kentucky	Kentucky State Board of Cosmetology	Cosmetologist	1,800	$12
	111 Saint James Court, #A	Nail technician	600	$10
	Frankfort, KY 40601			
	502-564-4262			
	fax: 502-564-0481			
	e-mail: dena.moore@mail.state.ky.us			
Louisiana	Louisiana Board of Cosmetology	Cosmetologist	1,500	$25
	11622 Sunbelt Court	Esthetician	750	$25
	Baton Rouge, LA 70809	Nail technician	500	$25
	225-756-3404	Massage therapist	500	$50
	fax: 225-756-3410			
	e-mail: lsbc@lsbc.state.la.us			
Maine	Maine State Board of Cosmetology	Cosmetologist	1,500 2,500 (apprentice)	$50
	Department of Professional Regulation			
	35 State House Station			
	Augusta, ME 04333	Esthetician	600 1,250 (apprentice)	$50
	207-624-8632			
	fax: 207-624-8637			
	e-mail: linda.s.harris@state.me.us	Nail technician	200 400 (apprentice)	$50
	www.maineprofessionalreg.org			
		Massage therapist	500	$100
Maryland	Maryland State Board of Cosmetologists	Cosmetologist	1,500 or 24 months apprenticeship	$25
	500 North Calvert Street, 3rd Floor			
	Baltimore, MD 21202			
	410-230-6320	Esthetician	600	$25
	fax: 410-333-6314	Nail technician	250	$25
	e-mail: mbrown@dllr.state.md.us			
	www.dllr.state.md.us			

STATE	CONTACT INFORMATION	AVAILABLE LICENSES	HOURS OF TRAINING REQUIRED	COST OF LICENSE
Massa-chusetts	Massachusetts Board of Cosmetology 239 Causeway Street Boston, MA 02114 617-727-3067 fax: 617-727-2197 www.state.ma.us/reg	Cosmetologist Electrologist Esthetician Nail technician	1,000 1,100 300 100	$25 $30 $25 $25
Michigan	Michigan Bureau of Commercial Services Board of Cosmetology P.O. Box 30018 Lansing, MI 48909-7518 517-241-9201 fax: 517-241-9280 e-mail: judy.dennis@cis.state.mi.us www.cis.state.mi.us	Cosmetologist Electrologist Esthetician Nail technician	1,500 400 400 400	$24 $24 $24 $24
Minnesota	Minnesota Department of Commerce Cosmetology Enforcement 85 East 7th Place St. Paul, MN 55101 651-297-3839 fax: 651-296-4328 e-mail: pamela.eftikides@state.mn.us www.commerce.state.mn.us	Cosmetologist Esthetician Nail technician	1,550 600 350	$45 $45 $45
Mississippi	Mississippi State Board of Cosmetology 3000 Old Canton Road, Suite 112 Jackson, MS 39216-5689 601-987-6837 fax: 601-987-6840 e-mail: sbutler@msbc.state.ms.us www.msbc.state.ms.us	Cosmetologist Esthetician Nail technician Massage therapist	1,550 600 250 600	$25 $25 $25
Missouri	Missouri State Board of Cosmetology 3605 Missouri Boulevard P.O. Box 1062 Jefferson City, MO 65102 573-751-1052 fax: 573-751-8167 e-mail: cosmo@mail.state.mo.us www.ecodev.state.mo.us/pr	Cosmetologist Esthetician Nail technician	1,500 600 350	$85 $85 $85

STATE	CONTACT INFORMATION	AVAILABLE LICENSES	HOURS OF TRAINING REQUIRED	COST OF LICENSE
Montana	Montana Board of Cosmetologists P.O. Box 200513 Helena, MT 59620-0513 406-841-2333 fax: 406-841-2305 e-mail: compolcos@state.mt.us www.discoveringmontana.com/dli/bsd/license/ bsd_boards/cos_board/licenses/cos/lic_summary.htm#e	Cosmetologist Electrologist Esthetician Nail technician	2,000 600 650 350	$45 $45 $45 $45
Nebraska	Nebraska Department of Health & Human Services 301 Centennial Mall South, 3rd Floor P.O. Box 94986 Lincoln, NE 68509 402-471-2117 fax: 402-417-3577 e-mail: kris.chiles@hhss.state.ne.us www.hhs.state.ne.us	Cosmetologist Electrologist Esthetician Massage therapist	2,100 600 600 1,000	$42 $42 $42 $252
Nevada	Nevada Board of Cosmetology 1785 East Sahara Avenue, #255 Las Vegas, NV 89104 702-486-6542 fax: 702-369-8064 e-mail: nvcosmbd@govmail.state.nv.us www.state.nv.us/cosmetology/	Cosmetologist Electrologist Esthetician Nail technician	1,800 500 600 500	$40 $40 $40 $40
New Hampshire	New Hampshire Board of Cosmetology and Esthetics 2 Industrial Park Drive Concord, NH 03301 603-271-3608 fax: 603-271-8889 e-mail: lelliott@nhsa.state.nh.us www.state.nh.us/cosmet/	Cosmetologist Esthetician Nail technician Massage therapist	1,400 450 150 750	$30 $30 $30 $50
New Jersey	New Jersey Board of Cosmetology 124 Halsey Street, 6th Floor Newark, NJ 07101 973-504-6400 fax: 973-648-3536 www.state.nj.us	Cosmetologist Electrologist Esthetician Nail technician	1,200 1,200 600 200	$60 $60 $60 $60

STATE	CONTACT INFORMATION	AVAILABLE LICENSES	HOURS OF TRAINING REQUIRED	COST OF LICENSE
New Mexico	New Mexico State Board of Barbers and Cosmetologists P.O. Box 25101 Santa Fe, NM 87504 505-476-7110 fax: 505-476-7118 www.rld.state.nm.us/b&c	Cosmetologist Electrologist Esthetician Nail technician Massage therapist	600 500 600 600 650	$20 $20 $20 $20 $125
New York	New York Department of State Division of Licensing Services 84 Holland Avenue Albany, NY 12208-3490 518-474-4429 fax: 518-473-6648 e-mail: licensing@dos.state.ny.us www.dos.state.ny.us/	Cosmetologist Esthetician Nail specialty Wax specialty	1,000 600 250 75	$20 $20 $20 $20
North Carolina	North Carolina Board of Cosmetology 1201 Front Street, #110 Raleigh, NC 27609 919-733-4117 fax: 919-733-4127 e-mail: ncs0963@mindspring.com www.cosmetology.state.nc.us	Cosmetologist Esthetician Nail technician Massage therapist	1,500 600 300 500	$33 $10 $10 $100
North Dakota	North Dakota Board of Cosmetology 1102 South Washington, #200 P.O. Box 2177 Bismarck, ND 58502 701-224-9800 fax: 701-222-8756 e-mail: cosmo@gcentral.com	Cosmetologist Esthetician Nail technician Massage therapist	1,800 900 350 750	$10 $15 $15 $30
Ohio	Ohio State Board of Cosmetology 101 Southland Mall Columbus, OH 43207-4041 614-644-6099 fax: 614-644-6880 e-mail: lavaughn.gearhart@cos.state.oh.us www.state.oh.us/cos/	Cosmetologist Esthetician Nail technician Massage therapist	1,500 600 200 600	$30 $30 $30 $50

STATE	CONTACT INFORMATION	AVAILABLE LICENSES	HOURS OF TRAINING REQUIRED	COST OF LICENSE
Oklahoma	Oklahoma State Board of Cosmetology 2200 Classen Boulevard, #1530 Oklahoma City, OK 73106 405-521-2441 fax: 405-528-8310 e-mail: bmoore@oklaosf.state.ok.us www.state.ok.us/~cosmo/	Cosmetologist Esthetician Nail technician	1,500 600 600	$15 $15 $15
Oregon	Oregon Health Licensing Agency 700 Summer Street NE #320 Salem, Oregon 97301-1287 503-378-8667 fax: 503-585-9114 e-mail: hlo.info@state.or.us www.hlo.state.or.us	Cosmetologist Electrologist Esthetician Massage therapist Nail technician	1,700 600 500 500 600	$35 $175 $35 $80 $35
Pennsylvania	Pennsylvania State Board of Cosmetology Professional & Occupational Affairs P.O. Box 2649 Harrisburg, PA 17105-2649 717-783-7130 fax: 717-705-5540 e-mail: cosmetol@pados.dos.state.pa.us www.dos.state.pa.us/	Cosmetologist Esthetician Nail technician	1,250 (school) 2,000 (apprentice) 300 200	$23 $21 $21
Puerto Rico	Puerto Rico Juntes Examinadoras P.O. Box 3271 Old Station San Juan, PR 00902 787-722-2122 fax: 787-722-4818	Cosmetologist	1,000	
Rhode Island	Rhode Island Department of Health Professional Regulation Board of Hairdressing 3 Capital Hill Providence, RI 02908 401-222-2827, ext. 113 fax: 401-222-1272 e-mail: lindaa@doh.state.ri.us www.health.state.ri.us	Cosmetologist Electrologist Esthetician Massage therapist Nail technician	1,500 650 600 500 300	$30 $25 $30 $25 $30

STATE	CONTACT INFORMATION	AVAILABLE LICENSES	HOURS OF TRAINING REQUIRED	COST OF LICENSE
South Carolina	South Carolina Board of Cosmetology 110 Centerview Drive, #104 P.O. Box 11329 Columbia, SC 29211-1329 803-896-4830 fax: 803-896-4484 e-mail: jonese@mail.llr.state.sc.us www.llr.state.sc.us/boc.htm	Cosmetologist Esthetician Massage therapist Nail technician	1,500 450 500 300	$15 $15 $200 $15
South Dakota	South Dakota Cosmetology Commission 500 East Capital Pierre, SD 57501 605-773-6193 fax: 605-773-7175 e-mail: cosmetology@state.sd.us www.state.sd.us/dcr/index.htm	Cosmetologist Nail technician	2,100 400	$15 $15
Tennessee	Tennessee State Board of Cosmetology 500 James Robertson Parkway, #130 Nashville, TN 37243-1147 615-741-2515 fax: 615-741-1310 e-mail: egriffin@mail.state.tn.us www.state.tn.us	Cosmetologist Esthetician Nail technician Massage therapist	1,500 750 600 500	$50 $50 $50 $260
Texas	Texas Cosmetology Commission P.O. Box 26700 Austin, TX 78755-0700 512-454-4674 fax: 512-454-0339 e-mail: diane.hill@txcc.state.tx.us www.txcc.state.tx.us	Cosmetologist Esthetician Nail technician Massage therapist	1,500 600 600 250	$43 $43 $43 $40

STATE	CONTACT INFORMATION	AVAILABLE LICENSES	HOURS OF TRAINING REQUIRED	COST OF LICENSE
Utah	Utah Division of Occupational and Professional Licensing Department of Commerce P.O. Box 146741 160 East 300 Street South Salt Lake City, Utah 84111-6741 801-530-6628 fax: 801-530-6511 e-mail: cormond@br.state.ut.us www.commerce.state.ut.us.dopl.dop	Cosmetologist Esthetician Nail technician	2,000 600 200	$50 $50 $50
Vermont	Vermont Office of Secretary of State Office of Professional Regulation Board of Barber & Cosmetologists 26 Terrace Street, Drawer 09 Montpelier, VT 05609-1106 802-828-2837 fax: 802-828-2465 e-mail: nmorin@sec.state.vt.us www.vtprofessionals.org	Cosmetologist Esthetician Nail technician	1,500 300 150	$45 $45 $45
Virginia	Virginia Board of Barbers & Cosmetology 3600 West Broad Street Richmond, VA 23230 804-367-8509 fax: 804-367-6295 e-mail: www.state.va.us/dpor/ cosmetology@dpor.state.va.us	Cosmetologist Nail technician Massage therapist	1,500 150 500	$25 $25 $50
Washington	Washington State Department of Licensing 405 Black Lake Boulevard P.O. Box 9026 Olympia, WA 98502-9026 360-586-4915 fax: 360-664-2550 e-mail: mschneider@dol.wa.gov www.dol.wa.gov/main/professional.htm	Cosmetologist Esthetician Nail technician Massage therapist	1,600 500 500 500	$40 $40 $40 $40

STATE	CONTACT INFORMATION	AVAILABLE LICENSES	HOURS OF TRAINING REQUIRED	COST OF LICENSE
West Virginia	West Virginia Board of Barbers and Cosmetologists 1716 Pennsylvania Avenue, #7 Charleston, WV 25302 304-558-2924 fax: 304-558-3450 e-mail: labsten@state.wv.us	Cosmetologist Esthetician Nail technician Massage therapist	2,000 600 400 500	$25 $25 $25 $100
Wisconsin	Wisconsin Department of Regulation and Licensing 1400 East Washington Avenue P.O. Box 8935 Madison, WI 53708-8935 608-266-5511 ext. 42 fax: 608-267-3816 e-mail: dorl@drl.state.wi.us www.drl.state.wi.us	Cosmetologist Electrologist Esthetician Massage therapist Nail technician	1,800 450 450 600 300	$63 $76 $87 $41 $133
Wyoming	Wyoming State Board of Cosmetology Hansen Building—East 2515 Warren Avenue, Suite 302 Cheyenne, WY 82002 307-777-3534 fax: 307-777-3681 e-mail: babern@state.wy.us www.state.wy.us	Cosmetologist Esthetician Nail technician	2,000 600 400	$36 $36 $36

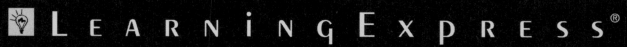

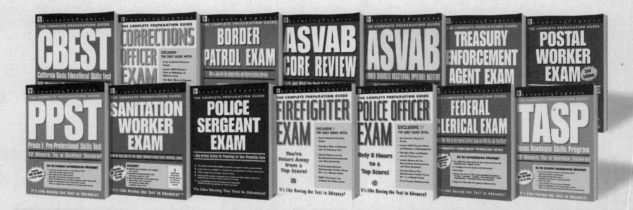